Revisiting the Essential Indexical

CSLI Lecture Notes Number 226

Revisiting the Essential Indexical

John Perry

CSLI
PUBLICATIONS
Center for the Study of
Language and Information
Stanford, California

Copyright © 2019
CSLI Publications
Center for the Study of Language and Information
Leland Stanford Junior University
Printed in the United States
23 22 21 20 19   1 2 3 4 5

Library of Congress Cataloging-in-Publication Data

Names: Perry, John, 1943- author.

Title: Revisiting the essential indexical / John Perry.

Description: Stanford : CSLI Publications, 2019. | Series: CSLI Lecture Notes ; 226
| Includes bibliographical references and index. | Summary:"In this book,
renowned philosopher John Perry addresses critiques of his work on the essential
indexical"– Provided by publisher.

Identifiers: LCCN 2019030298 | ISBN 9781684000524 (paperback) |
ISBN 9781684000616 (cloth) | ISBN 9781684000531 (ebook)

Subjects: LCSH: Meaning (Philosophy) | Indexicals (Semantics)

Classification: LCC B105.M4 P4775 2019 | DDC 121/.68–dc23

LC record available at https://lccn.loc.gov/2019030298

CIP

∞ The acid-free paper used in this book meets the minimum requirements of the
American National Standard for Information Sciences—Permanence of Paper for
Printed Library Materials, ANSI Z39.48-1984.

CSLI Publications is located on the campus of Stanford University.

Visit our web site at
http://cslipublications.stanford.edu/
for comments on this and other titles, as well as for changes
and corrections by the author and publisher.

In memory of
Ken Taylor
1954–2019
Colleague, Friend, and Brilliant Philosopher

"Question everything!"

—*Philosophy Talk*

Contents

... there is no such thing as essential indexicality, irreducibly *de se* attitudes, or self-locating attitudes. Our goal is not to show that we need to rethink these phenomena –that they should be explained in ways different from how, e.g., Lewis and Perry explained them. Our goal is to show that the entire topic is an illusion – there's nothing there.
– Herman Cappelen and Josh Dever, *The Inessential Indexical* (2013, p. 3)

... [Cappelen and Dever's] book promotes a retrograde movement in philosophy, but the judicious reader who consults the original work will discover this. The best way to usher in the era of the essential indexical is for everyone to read this book and realize it caricatures the original arguments.... Once we realize the original arguments of Lewis and Perry (and Chisholm) survive Cappelen's and Dever's onslaught, we can direct our attention to the philosophy of human selfhood growing from the essential indexical.
– Arthur Falk, *Hermann Cappelen and Josh Dever, The Inessential Indexical* (2015, p. 429)

1

Introduction*

My articles "Frege on Demonstratives" (1977) and "The Problem of the Essential Indexical" (1979) are the main targets of Herman Cappelen and Josh Dever's book, *The Inessential Indexical* (2013), and presumably the latter essay was the inspiration for its title. In the book, they claim that (i) I did not articulate a clear thesis in these papers, (ii) the terminology I introduce is not well defined, and (iii) I develop no interesting or powerful arguments for this unclear thesis couched in ill-defined terminology, which they call "the thesis of Essential Indexicality" or "Essential Indexicality." Forty years after writing the essays, I certainly see ways they might have been improved, but I think Ceppelen and Dever's verdict is a bit harsh.

I harbored hopes that reviewers of the book would defend me against some of Cappelen and Dever's criticisms. Philip Atkins (2016) makes the key point that their "attempt to subsume Perry's point about indexicals under the more general principle that co-referring expressions can't be substituted *salva veritate* in certain contexts" is mistaken. But it still seemed that the defense of me was going to be mainly up to me.

After I got started, Maria de Ponte and Kepa Korta discovered a very insightful review by Arthur Falk, from which the quotation above is taken (Falk 2015). He also wrote a longer essay on these

* Many thanks to Ken Taylor, Dikran Karagueuzian, Sarah Weaver, Russell Perry, Ken Perry, François Recanati, and the members of the International Zoom Group to which I belong for valuable comments.

issues, which he doesn't seem to have published before his death in 2018. It was very encouraging to have the support of an astute philosopher from my generation, and I have benefitted greatly from points Falk made in these essays.

Other reviewers make important criticisms of Cappelen and Dever. Wolfram Hinzen (2015) explores the puzzling aspects of their last chapter, where they see a connection between pronouns, perspective, and subjectivity that is hard, or perhaps impossible, to understand. Juliana Faccio Lima (2018) offers convincing criticisms of their "action inventory" model.

Forty years later, I think I understand the historical context of my articles a bit better and perhaps can explain what I said a bit better. But I haven't found any reason to change the views I put forward in those papers and have developed over the many years since they were written. Although this book mainly deals with Cappelen and Dever's criticisms, it is not confined to discussing their views, but goes into various issues raised in ways that put them in wider contexts. And, to be honest, it goes into various issues I was in the mood to think and write about. This made it more fun to write, and I hope it will make it more interesting to read.

1   Plan

I start in Chapter 2 by explaining the conclusions of my articles, which often received much less attention than the examples that I used to motivate them. Then I turn to "Frege on Demonstratives" and "The Problem of the Essential Indexical," where I first argued for these views.

In Chapters 3–7, I turn to opacity and cognitive significance. I think that confusion on these topics is the leitmotif of *The Inessential Indexical*. I extract a challenge about cognitive significance from some rather confusing criticisms and respond to it. Chapter 7 is a bit of a digression; I discuss some approaches to the problem I didn't discuss in the essays, and about which, in spite of its prominence in their book, Cappelen and Dever tell us very little: opacity. Chapters 8 deals with Cappelen and Dever's rather bewildering discussion of my case of Hume and Heimson. In Chapters 9 and 10, I discuss arguments they offer dealing with Arthur Prior and Saul Kripke and related issues that arise from the works of these authors. In Chapter 11, I return to the topic of self-knowledge, the issue that motivated the two original papers, which comes up in a couple of places in *The Inessential Indexical*. I then try (in vain) to understand what Cappelen and Dever are driving at in their final chapter, "The View From Everywhere." Then I come to a conclusion.

2

The Basic Claims

1 Solution

Some readers seem so fascinated with the title of "The Problem of the Essential Indexical" and the examples I give at the beginning of the paper that they don't seem to have taken the time to study the solution to the problem I offer at the end. Here I'll start with the solution.

My solution was to give up the "doctrine of propositions," or more precisely, to amend the first tenet, keep the second, and reject the third. The three tenets are:

(1) Beliefs (and other cognitive attitudes) *consist in* relations to the propositions referred to by the 'that'-clauses of attitude reports of the form "X believes that S." S is the *embedded sentence.* [1]

(2) The truth-values of propositions do not depend on who asserts them or believes them, or when.

(3) If X believes the proposition that S, that belief will lead X to regard S as true. That is, the proposition not only captures the truth-conditions of S, but also its cognitive content or cognitive significance, the beliefs that lead one to regard it as true.

The problem to be solved, posed by the sentences with indexicals in the examples in the two essays, was that neither of the two leading candidates for the propositions to which 'that'-clauses refer can fulfill tenet (3).

---

1. I've added the words "consist in" to the original formulation for clarification. I did not deny that there is an induced relation between believers and propositions.

- On basically Fregean theories, we have qualitative or general propositions, such as Frege's Thoughts.[2] But I argued that there is no such proposition belief in which explains why a certain person at a certain time will regard "I am making a mess" or "That is Lake Gilmore" to be true.[3]

- In the new theories of reference developed in the sixties and seventies and since, including David Kaplan's theory of indexicals, singular propositions are usually seen as the references of 'that'-clauses using names or indexicals. Singular propositions cannot even capture the differences is cognitive significance between "Cicero was an orator" and "Tully was an orator."

- One approach is to claim that for one reason or another, this really isn't a problem for semantics. This is somewhat plausible where proper names are the issue. But sentences with indexicals pose an additional problem, or a more serious version of the problem, because on Kaplan's extremely plausible theory, their semantics does seem to explain their cognitive significance (1979; 1989). But this cognitive significance is not captured by the singular propositions which are the contents of the embedded sentences on his account.

My solution was to amend tenet (1) and abandon tenet (3), thus "unburdening" propositions and accounts of the semantics of attitude reports. Belief and other attitudes do not *consist in* relations to propositions, but in having various mental episodes occur in the brain and central nervous system of an agent at a time. The truth-conditions of such episodes depend on the circumstances of the agent at the time as well as the nature of the inner episodes. There is a relation between beliefs and the propositions that capture their truth-conditions, but beliefs don't *consist in* having such a relation to these abstract objects.

Belief reports classify beliefs in terms of their truth-conditions, not in terms of the types of the belief episodes that are involved. That

---

2. I capitalize the word 'thought' when it is used as Frege did, as a translation of "Gedanken" used in his special way, and make the change in the translations from which I quote.

3. This claim is qualified in Chapter 5.

is, belief reports are concerned with *what* is believed, not *how* it is believed. The choice of the embedded sentence will often suggest something about how the belief is held, however. If X regards "Cicero was an orator" as true and does not so regard "Tully was an orator," it will be misleading, but true, to say "X believes Tully was an orator." If X has just come to correctly regard "That is Lake Gilmore" as true, it will be misleading to report this as "X has just come to believe that Lake Gilmore is Lake Gilmore."

We can classify types of belief episodes so as to capture their cognitive significance with *roles* (in "Frege on Demonstratives") or *relativized propositions* (in "The Problem of the Essential Indexical"). These are generalizations of Kaplan's concept of *characters* developed in "On the Logic of Demonstratives" (1979) and "Demonstratives" (1989). Characters are functions from agents, locations, times, and circumstances associated with expressions and sentences by the conventions of language. Roles are functions from agents, locations, times, and circumstances associated with types of belief episodes in virtue of their causal roles. Relativized propositions are simply an alternative way of thinking of roles.

Distinguishing between *what* is believed and *how* it is believed fits with common sense. We distinguish between what is perceived and how it is perceived, and what is done and how it is done. It makes sense that we should make a similar distinction with belief.

My solution did not involve anything I called "essentially indexicality" or "the thesis of the essential indexical." Examples with indexicals posed the problem. Kaplan's theory of indexicals suggested an important part of the solution. However, indexicals don't *explain* but rather *reflect* the pervasive distinction between *how* and *what* that is the basis of the solution. The distinction is the basis of the evolution of cognition. Different animals of the same species at different times can be in the same inner states and make the same kinds of movements. They thereby perceive different things, have beliefs or some precursors of beliefs about different things, and bring about different results when they execute the movements. This didn't happen because Mother Nature read "On the Logic of Demonstratives." It's hard to see how else She could have done it.

2   "Frege on Demonstratives"

"Frege on Demonstratives" and "The Problem of the Essential Indexical" began as parts of a long paper I wrote towards the end of a sabbatical I had in 1974 and eventually split in two on the advice of Julius Moravcsik. He wisely observed that the paper was too long to be published but could be divided into one aimed at Frege's theory and another focused on the new theories of reference emerging from works by Keith Donnellan (1966; 1970), Saul Kripke (1980), David Kaplan, and others.

I had spent the year studying Sydney Shoemaker's (1963; 1968) works on personal identity, essays by Hector-Neri Castañeda (1966; 1967; 1968) that Harry Deutsch had brought to my attention, my mimeographed copy of David Kaplan's (1979) "On the Logic of Demonstratives," and my worn copy of Peter Geach and Max Black's (1960) *Translations from the Philosophical Writings of Gottlob Frege*, my bible since graduate school, along with "The Thought" (1956) and a couple of other essays not included in Geach and Black. I wanted to understand self-knowledge, and was sure I could glean the answers from these works.

The solution I came up with, after many months of frustration, basically involved changing the order of quantifiers in something Frege said in "The Thought" (1956):

> Now everyone is presented to himself in a particular and primitive way, in which he is presented to no one else. So, when Dr. Lauben thinks that he has been wounded, he will probably take as a basis this primitive way in which he is presented to himself. And only Dr. Lauben himself can grasp Thoughts determined in this way. (298)

It's pretty clear from the rest of the passage that Frege had this order of the quantifiers in mind:

> For each person, there is a particular and primitive way in which he is presented to himself and no one else ... and no one else can grasp

Thoughts determined in this way.

That is, each person has Thoughts about herself or himself via a special primitive mode of presentation or sense that determines that person as reference. Others cannot grasp that sense, or Thoughts with it as a component. It was hard for me to come up with a plausible account of these senses; I thought Frege's appeal to what I call senses and Thoughts of "limited accessibility" was contrary to the spirit of his realm of Thoughts. It was only with great reluctance that I concluded Frege wasn't right about something.

I thought we could obtain the correct view of self-knowledge, however, if we reverse the order:

> There is a particular and primitive way in which every person is presented to himself, and no one else.

I think Frege had in mind that Dr. Lauben discovers he has been wounded by feeling the injury. Perhaps he was shot in the arm in battle. I think anyone might be aware of a similar injury in basically the same way, by having the same sort of sensation. It seemed to me they would also have the same sort of thought or Thought, and this sufficed to explain why they would react in the same way – among other things, saying "I have been injured."

But when Dr. Lauben says "I have been injured," he refers to himself; when his comrade utters the same words he doesn't refer to Dr. Lauben, but to himself. And each expresses a thought about themselves. If we all are presented to ourselves in the same *way*, what makes the thoughts we have in virtue of such presentations about us? They will not be complete Fregean Thoughts. You and I both feel a pain and have beliefs naturally expressed with "I am in pain." We say different things in the same way. With the quantifiers in Frege's order, however, we will not believe things in the same way. We grasp Thoughts via grasping the senses involved in them. Your belief will involve grasping a Thought involving your particular and primitive sense, and my belief will involve my grasping a Thought involving my particular and primitive sense. But if we are both presented to ourselves in the same way, with no special and primitive sense involved, we seem to grasp only partial Thoughts, with nothing in them to reflect who has to be in pain for them to be true.

At this point, I thought Kaplan's theory of demonstratives and indexicals provided the answer. On his theory, the word 'I' has as its meaning a *character*, which is a function from a context to a referent or "content." A context consists of an agent, location, time, and possible world; in a *proper* context, the agent is at the location at the time in the world. The character of 'I' takes us from the pair consisting of that expression and a context C to the agent of C. There are no utterances in Kaplan's formal theory. Thus we can say that "I am here now" is true in every proper context: it is a theorem in the logic of demonstratives. When we apply the theory to utterances, the context consists of the speaker, location, time, and place of the utterance.

The content of a sentence containing names, indexicals, or demonstratives in Kaplan's theory is a singular proposition. In the example, your utterance of "I am in pain" and mine have the same character, but you express a singular proposition with you as a constituent, and I express one with me as a constituent. I generalized Kaplan's theory to beliefs. Just as there were sentences that could be used to say different things, by different people or at different times, there were *ways of believing* that constituted believing different things for different people or at different times. In these cases, *what* was believed wouldn't be a Fregean Thought, but a singular proposition.

To apply Kaplan's theory, I introduced the term 'role' for my generalization of characters. At the time, I thought the possible worlds framework, which I preferred to avoid, was more intrinsic to his theory than it was, so simply using his terminology seemed to be misleading. In addition, Kaplan had expressed, in the nicest way possible, some justified fears that I might go off half-cocked and apply his theory all over the place; since that's what I was doing, I thought it best not to steal his terminology for my possibly half-baked generalization in a somewhat different framework.

When we understand a word like "today," what we seem to know is a rule taking us from an occasion of utterance to a certain object. "Today" takes us to the very day of utterance, "yesterday" to the day before the day of utterance, "I" to the speaker, and so forth. I shall call this the *role* of the demonstrative.

I then used 'role' for the functions that take different people at different times who are in the same belief state to different things believed.

So the basic argument of the essay is the one presented above: there are ways of believing, and different people at different times can believe different things in the same way, with the difference in *what* they believe being ultimately due to who is doing the believing and when, rather than a special and incommunicable sense that each has for themselves.

I then argued that we could use this distinction to provide a more plausible view of Frege's theory of sense and reference.

Frege had two ways of classifying sentences: by the Thoughts they express, and by their truth-values. I thought he needed two more ways. First, he needed singular propositions, a close cousin of the circumstances he had countenanced in his *Begriffsschrift*. Frege abandoned such propositions because he rightly saw that they could not explain differences in cognitive significance between sentences with co-referring expressions. But I think they are needed because they explain what such sentences have in common, by requiring the same objects to have the same properties. It is this that is essential to understanding communication of information and storage of information even within a single mind. Second, he needed roles to account for the ways that we each acquire information about ourselves and the ways in which we gather information about what is happening at that time. The two additions are connected, because roles in context give us singular propositions, not complete Thoughts.

I thought the resulting theory was pretty Fregean. But there is no gainsaying that to accept my view, and reverse the quantifiers in Frege's account of Dr. Lauben, one has to modify an important part of

Frege's picture; one has to give up an important tenet of the doctrine of propositions. As I understand his view, beliefs – episodes in the mental realm – have the truth-conditions that they do *in virtue of* the propositions we grasp in having them. That is part of the doctrine of propositions, in my terms.

On my view, the job of propositions is to encode the truth-conditions of our beliefs. In my view, it makes sense that facts about the episode – in particular, the agent and the time of the episode of belief – can play a role in determining its truth-conditions. As I understand Frege, grasping "I" Thoughts occurs not only when perfect languages suitable for science are involved, but also when the imperfect languages of everyday life are involved, and indeed when no language is involved. A pre-linguistic child who feels pain and believes that he is in pain and has been hurt will differ in many ways from Dr. Lauben. But they will have one thing in common: they know of the pain by feeling it. When they know of a pain in this way, and have a notion of themselves, they will believe themselves to be in pain.

As I said, I regard my theory as Fregean. I would call in "neo-Fregean" had that phrase not been co-opted for another set of views, which, as far as I can see, depart from Frege at least as far as mine does – indeed, further.

Be that as it may, my proposals didn't exactly attract universal applause. I return to some of the interpretive issues in *Frege's Detour* (2019), but won't dwell on them them in this book.

3 "The Problem of the Essential Indexical"

In "Demonstratives" (1989), Kaplan gives us his typology for indexicals and demonstratives. Indexicals are the top category. Under that heading we find demonstratives and "pure" indexicals. At the time I wrote "Frege on Demonstratives," I thought the top heading was "Demonstratives," because this word was in the title of "On the Logic of Demonstratives," and I knew it was the title he planned for the monograph he was working on. However, before finishing "The Problem of the Essential Indexical," I learned in conversation that he liked 'demonstratives' for his titles because it sounded better than 'indexicals', but his typology was that just explained. That's why the second article wasn't titled "The Problem of the Essential Demonstrative." There is no other significance to the change.

This made it possible to borrow the phrase 'essential indexical' from Hector-Neri Castañeda. He used it for indexicals than cannot be paraphrased away, even in terms of other indexicals. According to Castañeda, the essential indexicals in this sense are 'I' and 'now,' and I agree that they are essential in this sense. 'Here', for example, can be paraphrased as 'the place I am at now'. I also had in mind that indexicals in general cannot, at least in many cases, be paraphrased away in favor of other types of expressions, especially names and descriptions, as some philosophers had assumed, and that they often seem to make a contribution to the thoughts disclosed that is lost when co-referential names or descriptions are substituted for them. I did not think of this as a "thesis;" I thought Castañeda's examples and discussion had put this beyond reasonable doubt.

I gave three examples to illustrate the problem. My messy shopper (me) says "I am making a mess" and "JP is making a mess." The two sentences have different cognitive significance; I am unlikely to regard one as true and not the other, but someone who didn't know my name might. The difference seems important. The truth of the first requires that the same person who is making the utterance is making the mess. It seems to explain *that* person stopping and straightening up the sack in a very direct way, in which the second does not, although it might serve as an explanation for those who know my name and recognize me.

My tardy professor says, at noon, "The department meeting starts now" and "The department meeting starts at noon." Only the first directly explains his rushing off. My lost hiker says "That is Lake Gilmore" and "Lake Gilmore is Lake Gilmore." Only the first explains his ability to use his map to find his way home.

It might have been a good idea to use Descartes' argument, "I think, therefore I am" as an example. "Descartes exists therefore Descartes exists" wouldn't have made the same impact.[4] When he published his *Discourse* and *Meditations*, he presumably wanted to encourage others to sink into skepticism, and then to start their way out by thinking in the same way he had, and see that since they thought they must exist. It was *how* Descartes thought, not the *what* he thought, that was important to this strategy.

In my three cases, the indexical seems to disclose something important about the belief that motivates the utterance. But this is unreflected in the singular proposition that serves as its *content* in Kaplan's sense, *what* is said. Suppose Fred says, "Cicero was an orator." I'll say that Fred *discloses* a belief with the *cognitive significance* of "Cicero was an orator" – that is, a belief that leads a competent speaker to regard this sentence as true. I'll say that Fred *expresses* the belief that Cicero was an orator; that is, a belief with the truth-conditions identified by the proposition *that Cicero was an orator*. And I'll say "Fred believes that Cicero was an orator" *reports* his having a belief in that proposition. On Frege's theory, the aspect of the belief disclosed is the same as that expressed or reported. On the singular propositions account, this is not so. Fred would disclose a different belief with "Tully was an orator" but would express the same proposition.

4 Varieties of Propositions

As I said above, I thought we needed to unburden singular propositions and appreciate them for what they do well: encode which objects have to have which properties and stand in which relations for an utterance or a belief to be true. We need to give up the central tenet of the doctrine of propositions – that belief and other attitudes *consist in* relations to propositions – thus unburdening propositions. Before getting to the solution, however, I wanted to show that the problem was not simply a problem for the new theory of reference and singular propositions, and one should not simply abandon that

---

4. As Anscombe makes clear in "The First Person" (1975).

view. I considered three alternatives: Fregean theories that took *what* is said and believed to be general propositions, theories of limited accessibility, and what I called the theory of relativized propositions. I'll have some things to say about the first two later, but I need to say a bit about the third here.

What I called a relativized proposition was basically a parametric proposition, with the elements of context as parameters. Corresponding to the character of 'you are eating,' we have a relativized proposition: the person a is talking to at t at l in w is eating at t in w. What if we simply take saying and believing and the other attitudes to *consist in* relation to relativized propositions? I raised an objection to this approach, which I'll return to when I discuss David Lewis's views. Interestingly, at the same time I was articulating the theory of relativized propositions in order to criticize it, Lewis (1979) was developing a similar theory. I could have simply called relativized propositions "properties" that an agent might have at a time in a world. Locations can be dispensed with, if Castañeda is right. Corresponding to characters, we have properties of an agent at a time in a world. Lewis took belief to consist in the "self-ascription" of such properties.

In explaining my solution to the problem of the essential indexical, I needed to generalize Kaplan's concept of a character to get at different ways of believing the same singular proposition. In "Frege on Demonstratives," I had introduced the concept of a *role* for this purpose. In "The Problem of the Essential Indexical," however, since I had already introduced relativized propositions, I used them for this purpose, probably trying to keep the essay short enough to be accepted for publication. In this use, the relative propositions were not *what* we believe, but simply abstract objects that classify belief states in terms of their causal roles and determine their truth-conditions, in conjunction with facts about the context of the belief.

To explain my alternative to the doctrine of propositions, I made a shift, somewhat dramatically I thought, between two kinds of cases.

For the purposes of this book, where the difference is often relevant to Cappelen and Dever's criticisms, I'll give them labels. Type B cases involve the same agent believing or asserting the same proposition in two different ways, with differing cognitive significance. The messy shopper, tardy professor, and lost hiker provided Type B cases. From the singular propositions point of view, the classic cases of differing cognitive significance are also Type B cases. "Tully was an orator" and "Cicero was an orator" are two ways of saying the same thing.

Type A cases involve different speakers and/or different times. The speakers say or believe different propositions in virtue of saying or believing in the same way. Kaplan's theory predicts and explains Type A cases. Different tardy professors, or the same tardy professor on different days, say different things, and disclose different beliefs with different contents, by saying "the department meeting starts now." The sentences mean the same, and disclose beliefs with the same causal role, but what is asserted and what is believed is different. I said:

> ... consider all the responsible professors who have ever uttered "The department meeting is starting now." They ... have something important in common; they are in a state that will lead those just down the hall to go to the meeting, those across campus to curse and feel guilty, those on leave to smile. (1979, p. 17)

So, in the last section of the essay, we have *lots* of potentially tardy professors saying and believing different things in the same way, rather than one tardy professor saying and believing the same thing in two different ways. The shift from Type B to Type A cases was intended to produce the insight that the characters of the sentences used, or the relativized propositions, really do get at something we naturally think these different believers who believe different things have in common, that motivates similar actions with different results, involving different professors setting out to different department meetings on different days.

Indexicals naturally give rise to Type A cases. What about proper names? In imperfect languages, we have what I call "nambiguity."

I say, "Aristotle liked syllogisms," saying something pretty obvious about the ancient logician. You say, "Aristotle liked syllogisms," saying something rather surprising about Jackie Kennedy's second husband. This is a Type A case, different things being said in the same way. For a long time, nambiguity was pretty much ignored; new theorists typically put such cases to one side in developing their accounts of proper names. It seems an accident about proper names that we have nambiguity, inessential to understanding the way proper names work, and so not very interesting. But, with indexicals, Type A cases are not accidents due to a form of ambiguity. They are a central phenomenon predicted by Kaplan's theory.

So that was my solution. Give up the central doctrine of the doctrine of propositions. Distinguish between *what* is believed and *how* it is believed. We use indexicals to disclose *how* we believe; singular propositions get at *what* we believe.

> ... Belief states must be distinguished from objects of belief, cannot be individuated in terms of them, and are what is crucial for the explanation of action ... (Perry 1979, p. 20)

If we accept this, we will understand why sentences with indexicals can disclose something important about beliefs not captured by singular propositions, which takes care of what I called "the problem of the essential indexical."

So, to sum up, I argued in "Frege on Demonstratives" that Frege needed singular propositions and roles in addition to Thoughts. And in "The Problem of the Essential Indexical," I argued that new theories of reference needed roles, as well as qualitative and singular propositions.

5 Some Boldfaced Claims

Cappelen and Dever seem to me to have been so inspired by the title of the article and its opening examples that they read that far and began free associating what I might be claiming, without pursuing the essay carefully through to the end. Cappelen and Dever put the products of this free association into a series of boldfaced claims that I didn't make. For example:

> **EI: Agency.** Chapter 3 explores the idea that indexicality (and 'the *de se*' in particular) plays an essential role in explaining and rationalizing action.

> **EI: Opacity.** Chapter 4 addresses the question of whether the presence of indexicals in (apparently) opaque contexts raises questions that are fundamentally and interestingly different from general issues about opacity.

As to **EI: Agency**, I did not claim that *indexicality* plays an essential role in explaining and rationalizing action, but that in particular cases *indexicals* did. I claimed that in the examples I gave, the expressions 'I,' 'now,' and 'that lake' were essential to the explanations given, because they lost their explanatory force without the indexicals. This feature of indexicals was the *explanandum*, not the *explanans*. What did the explaining was the distinction between the how and the what, between belief states and what is believed. One might call this pattern "indexicality," and I did at least once in the essay, but once I saw the confusions to which it led, I tried to avoid it and reserve "indexical" for a characteristic of certain expressions in language. (I'm not sure what "the *de se*" means.) Using indexicals exhibits a pattern – the distinction between *how* one does something and *what* one does in that way – that certainly plays an essential role in explaining and rationalizing action, recognized by (almost) any theory of action.

My use of the term "essential" had to do with particular examples; the use of a 'I' or 'now' or 'that lake' seemed to play a key role in the sentences the messy shopper, the tardy professor, and the lost hiker used to explain their actions. I made no claim that they or someone else couldn't explain their actions in some other way, much less that all explanations and rationalizations of actions require indexicals.

EI: Opacity is more mystifying. I did not discuss opacity. The word does not appear in either essay. I considered different theories of propositions, some of which are subscribed to by those who believe in opacity; other theories, such as the singular propositions view that I favored, typically lead to denying opacity. I claimed that the essential indexical examples are problems for both theories of propositions but did not discuss their differences as regards opacity. While my Type B examples can be converted into illustrations of opacity or the appearance of opacity, Type A examples – the ones that do the work in explaining my solution – cannot be.

So this leads to my fundamental claim in this book:

The Confusion: Cappelen and Dever confuse opacity with cognitive significance. This is the leitmotif of their book and the basis of most of their criticisms. But, as they might put it, there is nothing there.

3

Opacity and Cognitive Significance

1 A Recurrent Theme

In Chapter 1 of *The Inessential Indexical*, Cappelen and Dever say:

> It is a familiar and much investigated fact that the principle of substitutivity of co-referential terms appears to fail in certain kinds of linguistic contexts. A recurrent theme in this work will be that much of what has been paraded as instances of essential indexicality is nothing but an instantiation of this (apparent) phenomenon. It should come as no surprise that indexicals behave like, e.g., proper names in this respect ... It looks like some form of opacity will always be needed as evidence for Essential Indexicality. (p. 28)

In Chapter 3 (p. 33), they say:

> Here is one way to summarize Perry's claim:
>
> **Indexical Opacity.** There's a set of indexicals, I-SET, that cannot be substituted *salva veritate* in action-explanation contexts by any other expressions.
>
> It should be clear that this is an instantiation of the more general thesis:
>
> **Generic Opacity.** Co-referential referring expressions cannot be substituted *salva veritate* in action-explanation contexts.

This is all quite puzzling.

This is what opacity is, according to the *Stanford Encyclopedia of Philosophy*:

> A sentence, or more accurately a position in a sentence, is held to be referentially transparent if terms or phrases in that position that refer to

the same object can be freely substituted without altering the truth of the sentence.

Sentences, or positions, are referentially opaque just in case they are not transparent, that is, if the substitution of co-referring terms or phrases could potentially alter their truth-value. (Schwitzgebel 2019)

What does opacity have to do with what I said in my essays?

Nothing. Any force that Cappelen and Dever's arguments may seem to have is an illusion.

None of my examples or arguments turned on substitution of indexicals changing the truth-value of the sentences. Nor did they turn on such substitutions changing the truth-value of reports in which the sentences occurred. In Kaplan's theory and mine, direct discourse and attitude reports are not opaque. My solution to the problem I posed was not to say that they were opaque, but in a special way, or that they were not opaque, but in a special way. As I said, the words "opaque" and "opacity" do not occur in the essay.

The hiker says, "That is Lake Gilmore." This is true. He would have said something true but trivial if he had said "Lake Gilmore is Lake Gilmore." The substitution of the name 'Lake Gilmore' for the demonstrative is substitution *salva veritate*, whether or not it changes the proposition expressed. But, at least by my lights, the new sentence does not do a very good job expressing what the hiker had just figured out, which motivated him to start moving, at least not without a lot of assumptions not included in my story.

Now suppose we embed these in attitude reports. The hiker says:

I believe that *that* is Lake Gilmore.

I believe that Lake Gilmore is Lake Gilmore.

The truth-values would not change. On Frege's account, substitutions of co-referring expressions change the truth-conditions of such reports and thus can change the truth-values. One can hardly deny that this is plausible, since it was accepted by most philosophers of language for about seventy-five years after he wrote "On Sense and Reference." By the time I wrote "The Problem of the Essential Indexical," Kripke and other new theorists of reference had raised doubts that Frege's diagnosis was correct, and opacity was no longer the consensus doctrine among philosophers of language. Direct reference and singular propositions were hot topics. Whether we accept singular propositions or stick with Frege, the second report is true, but it tells us what the hiker believed all along and everyone who knows there is a lake called "Lake Gilmore" believes. Quite apart from the issue of opacity, the second report is not a very good explanation of his change of behavior. I argued that my examples posed a problem for the doctrine of propositions, whatever one took propositions to be, and whether or not one's account made attitude reports opaque.

The disconnection between opacity and what I was getting at comes out clearly in "The Obvious Solution," the last section of my second essay. Here I change from the Type B cases I used to state the problem to the Type A cases I use to motivate the solution. It is clear that Type A cases have nothing to do with opacity. Sitting in my office at Stanford, I look at my watch and have a thought I express with, "The department meeting is starting now." Sitting in his office at Berkeley, years earlier, John Searle looks at his watch and has a thought he expresses with, "The department meeting is starting now." We are both motivated get up and go to the relevant meeting. Opacity is nowhere on the horizon. Suppose we are asked why we are leaving. I say, "I believe that the department meeting is starting now." Searle says, "I believe that the department meeting is starting now." Now we at least have belief reports to deal with, but not opacity. My point is that, embedded or unembedded, the sentence "The department meeting is starting now" discloses a belief state we have in common, which, together with the desire state we are in as responsible professors, leads us to get up and starting moving. Opacity has nothing to do with it.

At one point in their book, Cappelen and Dever consider the Type A case I presented in "Frege on Demonstratives." David Hume and my fictional, somewhat confused, graduate student Heimson both sincerely say, "I am David Hume." They say different things in the same way, a Type A case. Cappelen and Dever see that the case has nothing to do with opacity. As we shall see below, at this point they punt. However, they present it as if they had scored a touchdown, or at least a field goal.

It is this fixation on opacity and disregard of Type A cases that leads to my hypothesis that they made it a ways through the article, began to free-associate on my apparently seductive title and examples, and never made it to my solution. I'm sure that's not the case, since they quote once or twice from the final section. But it is a useful heuristic.

2 Opacity and Cognitive Significance

In "The Problem of the Essential Indexical," I argued that neither Fregean Thoughts nor singular propositions explain the phenomenon of the essential indexical. Although I accepted Kaplan's theory and with it non-opacity, the problem I posed did not rely on either opacity or transparency. I was interested in differences of *cognitive significance*, my term for what Frege called "cognitive value." This was basically the beliefs a competent speaker must have in order to regard a sentence as true.

Cappelen and Dever simply confuse the issue of opacity and the issue of cognitive significance, repeatedly, often in boldface. Recall the second passage quoted above, from Chapter 3 (p. 33):

> Here is one way to summarize Perry's claim:
>
> **Indexical Opacity.**   There's a set of indexicals, I-SET, that cannot be substituted *salva veritate* in action-explanation contexts by any other expressions.
>
> It should be clear that this is an instantiation of the more general thesis:
>
> **Generic Opacity.** Co-referential referring expressions cannot be substituted *salva veritate* in action-explanation contexts.

They seem to be using "opacity" in the normal way; they speak of substitution "*salva veritate* in action-explanation contexts." But then things get very puzzling.

Their next step is to argue that *Generic Opacity* is true, with a "Fregean Counterpart," an example which doesn't involve indexicals. For simplicity, I'll take the shopper in their example to be me. This time I believe that Clark Kent is the messy shopper, but I don't realize that Superman is Clark Kent. Once I realize that, I tell Superman to quit making a mess.

But the conclusion they draw from the example is *not* Generic Opacity, but something quite different.

> We take the [this] case as showing that in general action explanations don't have their explanatory force preserved by substitution of co-referential singular terms. Seeing Indexical Opacity as an instance of Generic Opacity suggests that there's nothing deeply central about indexicals here. (p. 33)

But opacity is not the phenomenon of substitution of co-referring expressions possibly resulting in a difference in *explanatory force*; rather it is the phenomenon of such substitution possibly resulting in a change in *truth-value*, hence "*salva veritate*." At this point, the attentive reader should be quite lost.

Suppose Lois Lane and I are shopping together. I leave our shopping cart to pursue Superman, who is dressed in a cape, blue tights, and external underwear, so we both recognize him. She asks why I am pursuing Superman and I say, "I believe Superman is making the mess." That would be a fine explanation, since she knows I don't like messes and am courageous enough to confront anyone who makes them, even Superman. But "I believe Clark Kent is making the mess" would not explain things to Lois even though *I* know that Clark Kent is Superman, so truth would be preserved.[5] The two belief reports have the same truth-value, whether or not the embedded sentences express different Thoughts, as Frege would think, or the same singular proposition, as new theorists of reference would think. But they differ in explanatory force. Opacity is irrelevant. Suppose I had merely said, "Superman is making a mess." That, too, would have been a fine

---

5. For those who don't read comic books, Lois Lane didn't know that Superman was Clark Kent.

explanation. But, at least for Lois Lane, "Clark Kent is making a mess" would not have been. The difference in explanatory force seems due to the difference between two true sentences, independently of whether they occur embedded in a belief report or on their own, and independently of any issues about opacity.

3   A Recurrent Confusion

The confusion between opacity and differences in cognitive significance pervades *The Inessential Indexical*. At the beginning of Chapter 4, the authors say:

> In Chapter 3 and in later chapters we repeatedly make the following kind of move: in response to some allegedly distinctive feature of indexicals, we say that it is just an instance of opacity. We shouldn't be surprised or think it distinctive of indexicals that they can't be substituted *salva veritate* with co-referential expressions in, e.g., belief contexts. If a context is such that substituting co-referential terms isn't guaranteed to preserve truth-value, then substituting an indexical referring to *o* for a non-indexical referring to the same object *o* can result in a change of truth-value. This shows nothing distinctive about indexicals and provides no evidence for any kind of Essential Indexicality thesis. (p. 58)

I would change the last sentence to: "This shows nothing whatsoever about any of Perry's claims in "The Problem of the Essential Indexical.""

4   Frege Puzzles and Cognitive Significance

Cappelen and Dever see a close association between opacity and what they call "Frege puzzle cases," as in this quote:

> We take it that the ease with which Frege counterparts can be generated makes at least a *prima facie* case that the Perry/Lewis/Prior-style cases simply are familiar substitution puzzles and that nothing new is brought out that distinguishes indexicals from other referring expressions with respect to opacity. Here, then, is our challenge to those who find such cases powerful: What, if anything, distinguishes these cases from Frege puzzle cases? (pp. 68-9)

Frege did not find opacity puzzling. It's not clear that we should even say that he believed in opacity. It depends on how we take this passage in the definition:

Sentences, or positions, are referentially opaque just in case they are not transparent, that is, if the substitution of co-referring terms or phrases could potentially alter their truth-value. (Schwitzgebel 2019)

On Frege's theory, "Tully" and "Cicero" ordinarily co-refer. But when they are in sentences embedded in indirect discourse or attitude reports, they do not. They refer to their ordinary senses, which are different. If we take "co-referring" to mean "ordinarily co-referring," Frege believed in opacity, and gave an explanation of it. If we take it to mean "co-referring as they occur in the position in the sentence in question," then he recognized the appearance of opacity but denied that it really occurred. On the second interpretation, both Frege and the new theory of reference agree that opacity is an illusion but offer different explanations for the illusion. On the first, Frege believed in opacity, but the new theory of reference does not. Quine introduced the term 'opacity,' so Frege did not explain his view with this term.[6] Rather than digging into exactly what Quine meant, I'll just stick with the first interpretation, which seems to fit with the way Cappelen and Dever use the term.

Whatever we take opacity to be, Frege thought his theory of sense, reference, and indirect reference dealt with it, end of story. What he might have found puzzling are the arguments in the new theories of reference in favor of transparency, and the idea that singular propositions are what we believe. Such arguments did not puzzle Frege because he never considered them. Had he considered them, he would have rejected them out of hand, since he thought there were no singular propositions to serve as the contents of assertions and attitudes.

Kaplan sometimes calls singular propositions "Russellian propositions." Bertrand Russell accepted propositions with objects as constituents, and he and Frege communicated about the issue. Frege rejected singular propositions; his version of propositions, which he calls "Thoughts," have no objects as constituents; they are what we

---

6. Thanks to Genoveva Marti for helpful conversations on this point.

now call "general" or "qualitative" propositions. In a famous letter to Russell, he denies that Mount Blanc, with all of its snowfields, could possibly be a constituent of a Thought or a proposition (1980, p. 163).

But at one time, thirty-five years before the letter, and a dozen years before the theory of sense and reference, Frege had accepted what were basically singular propositions.

In his *Begriffsschrift* (1879), Frege took sentences to have *conceptual contents*, which involved circumstances: the circumstance of an object falling under a property (concept) or of a property falling under a higher-level property (and similarly for relations). For simplicity, I'll use the term 'circumstance' only for those involving objects. Such circumstances are a species of singular propositions. "Circumstance" was not a technical term for Frege, but simply the term he sometimes found natural in explaining his view of conceptual content.[7]

This led to a problem, for if "A = B" is true, it will stand for the same circumstance as "A = A", the circumstance individuated by the object named by both 'A' and 'B' and the relation of identity. But the first is synthetic, the second analytic. The two sentences do not license the same inferences, which he thought that sentences with the same conceptual content should do. In §8 of the *Begriffsschrift*, Frege basically retired '=' in favor of '≡'. "A ≡ B," contrary to appearances, is about the names 'A' and 'B' and is true if those names co-refer. We can conclude "A ≡ B" and "A ≡ A" do not stand for the same circumstance and do not have the same conceptual content. Frege's *Begriffsschrift* version of Leibniz's principle is

$$c \equiv d \rightarrow [f(c) \rightarrow f(d)]^{(8)}$$

By the time he wrote "Function and Concept" twelve years later,

---

7. This is a bit of an oversimplification. For example, he thinks that "Caesar conquered Gaul" and "Gaul was conquered by Caesar" have the same circumstance as their conceptual content, although the relation involved in the second is the inverse of that in the first. See *Frege's Detour* for further discussion.

8. In his notation,

Frege had realized the problem was not with '=' but with identity and circumstances, and the issue was broader than analyticity:

> If we say "The Evening Star is a planet with a shorter period of revolution than the Earth," the Thought we express is not the same one we express with "The Morning Star is a planet with a shorter period of revolution than the Earth." Someone who does not know that the Morning Star is the Evening Star might regard one as true and the other as false. (Frege 1960a, p. 29)

Both sentences are true. Neither sentence is analytic. The sentences do not contain '=' and don't assert identity, therefore they aren't handled by Frege's *Begriffsschrift* solution. But they license different inferences. In "On Sense and Reference," Frege says that such sentences have different "cognitive values." The substitution changes the cognitive value, but not the truth-value. I use the term that has become customary, "cognitive significance," which I gloss as the beliefs to which a semantically competent and sincere speaker is committed in uttering a sentence assertively, and that which a semantically competent and credulous hearer will come to believe from the utterance.

So there are two kinds of "Frege Puzzles." The first, which led to §8 of the *Begriffsschrift* and is recalled in the first paragraph of "On Sense and Reference," has to do with '='. The second, to which he immediately turns in "On Sense and Reference," has to do with the more general problem of "cognitive content" or "cognitive significance." It has nothing in particular to do with '=' but has to do with identity.[9] Neither problem is opacity, at least as the term is defined and (almost) universally understood. It is not that substitution of "The Morning Star" for "The Evening Star" leads to a sentence with a different *truth* value. The problem is that it leads to a sentence with a different *cognitive* value. If "The morning star has no moons" is true, "The evening star has no moons" is true. If "Cicero was an orator" is true, "Tully was an orator" is true. And, it seems, if my utterance of "I am making a mess" is true, then "JP is making a mess" is true. But the

---

9. Actually, the problem can be generated with any neccessarily reflexive relation, as George Wilson observed in 1967.

pairs of sentences have different cognitive significance.[10]

Once he saw the true nature of the problem, and realized that '≡' didn't solve it, Frege concluded that the real problem was not '=' but circumstances – contents that are individuated by objects. He then replaced conceptual contents with his theory of sense and reference. The sign '=' returns. Circumstances, and anything like singular propositions, disappear from Frege's work. It is Thoughts, not circumstances, that capture the cognitive significance of sentences, and there are no "singular" Thoughts. Frege's puzzles had ceased to puzzle Frege before he said anything about the substitution of singular terms in indirect discourse and attitude reports.

Thus the phenomenon of differences in cognitive significance is related to, but distinct from, the phenomenon of opacity, or apparent opacity. The new theories of reference, especially the claim that the the contents of beliefs and assertions are singular propositions, cannot be understood if one conflates them.

5   What Didn't Puzzle Frege

In "On Sense and Reference," Frege clearly thought that singular terms in direct reference and attitude reports were opaque, given the definition I have adopted. He did not find this puzzling at all. It was not a problem, but an opportunity. In his *Grundlagen* (1884), written between the *Begriffsschrift* and the essays that put forward the theory of sense and reference, Frege had arrived at the outlines of the strategy for the reduction of arithmetic to logic he was to attempt in his *Grundgesetze*. He saw that treating sentences as referring to truth-values would work well with the strategy. It allowed streamlining; principles of substitution needed for the (non-opaque) contexts of logic and arithmetic could apply to both names and sentences.

That clearly won't work for indirect discourse and attitude reports; we cannot substitute one sentence for another with the same truth-value in such reports and be assured of preserving the truth-value

---

10. So I basically use "Frege's Puzzle" as Nathan Salmon does, in his important book *Frege's Puzzle* (1986).

of the whole report. But, Frege thought, this was nicely handled by his theory of sense and reference; such sentences and the terms in them do not have their customary reference, but refer to their customary sense. The equipment he provided to deal with problem of cognitive significance allowed him to stick with truth-values as the ordinary references of sentences and handle opacity with the doctrine of indirect reference. This allowed him to set such reports aside as irrelevant to his dominant interest at the time, logic and the foundations of arithmetic. Opacity was a gift, not a puzzle, fitting nicely with his theory of sense and reference, and allowing him to exploit the simplifications in the theory of reference engendered by taking truth-values to be the references of sentences in his *Grundgesteze* where he didn't worry about attitudes or indirect discourse. While the *Grundgesetze* didn't quite work out as Frege had hoped, these simplifications in the theory of reference live on in logic as the truth-functionality and extensionality of the language of first-order logic.

4

Names and Indexicals: New Theories of Reference

1   Finding a Challenge

In this chapter and the next, I return to the principles that Cappelen and Dever attributed to me in Chapter 3 of *The Inessential Indexical*. I try to provide a charitable interpretation of what they may have been getting at, and then respond to the challenge they pose on this interpretation, from the perspective of new theories of reference in this chapter, and from a Fregean perspective in the next. I'll repeat the principles:

Indexical Opacity.   There's a set of indexicals, I-SET, that cannot be substituted *salva veritate* in action-explanation contexts by any other expressions.

Generic Opacity.   Co-referential referring expressions cannot be substituted *salva veritate* in action-explanation contexts.

Let's take it that they really had cognitive significance in mind, as charity and their following remark about "explanatory force" suggest.[11] Then the principles can be correctly labelled, re-formulated and properly boldfaced as:

Indexicals and Cognitive Significance.
Substituting indexicals with co-referential expressions may change the cognitive significance of the sentences in which they occur, including their explanatory force.

---

11. By "really" I simply mean according to the most charitable and coherent interpretation I can find.

Referring Expressions and Cognitive Significance. Substituting any referring expressions with co-referential expressions may change the cognitive significance of the sentences in which they occur, including their explanatory force.

These principles seem reasonable. Given this, the challenge they really wanted to pose to me and others who believe in "essential indexicality" is to show that there is anything special about indexicals as opposed to referring expressions in general, with respect to changes in cognitive significance resulting from such substitutions, especially in explanatory situations. I want to respond to this challenge.

To answer these questions, we need to consider how indexicals and proper names do their job of referring, to see if there are any differences that might be make indexicals special in this regard.

2   Losing What Is Specific

The new theories of reference I shall examine are singular proposition-alist, to coin an ugly phrase, with respect to both names and indexicals; I'll begin by saying a bit more about singular propositionalism.

Frege says in "On Sense and Reference" that in the reference of a sentence, all that is specific is lost. The reference of a sentence is a truth-value. Sentences as diverse as "Tully was an orator" and "The earth's orbit is elliptical" refer to the same thing, the truth-value True. The differences in subject matter are not reflected at the level of reference.

This was not a problem for Frege, since all that is specific is not lost at the level of sense and Thought. In contexts like indirect discourse and attitude reports, expressions and sentences do not refer to truth-values but to senses and Thoughts, their indirect references. One can say that on Frege's theory, all that is specific is not lost in the contents of assertions and attitudes, or in the references of embedded sentences in attitude reports. In particular, the differences in "modes of presentation" that give rise to differences in cognitive significance are not lost. In his theory, there is a close relation between cognitive significance and opacity. The connection disappears in the new theories of reference.

Singular propositions don't lose everything specific that truth-values lose. "Cicero was an orator" and "Cato was an orator" have the same truth-value but express different singular propositions. And if the singular propositionalist wants the ordinary reference of sentences to be truth-values, she can embrace Frege's doctrine of indirect reference, taking singular propositions to be the reference of suitably embedded sentences involving names and indexicals. But something important *is* lost with singular propositions: the ways the objects are identified and hence differences in cognitive significance. And we can't recover this lost specificity at the level of indirect reference, as on Frege's theory. In a singular proposition, we have objects, not modes of presentation, senses, individual concepts, characters, or anything else that marks the differences between singular terms that refer to the same thing and might give rise to differences in cognitive significance between two sentences whose truth conditions put the same demands on the same objects. In the messy shopper incident, the content of my assertion "I am making a mess," my wife's assertion "You are making a mess," and the assertions of "JP is making a mess" or "He is making a mess" with a demonstration towards me by others in the the store at the time all express the same singular proposition, that JP is making a mess.

This presents problems, which cannot be recognized if we conflate opacity and differences in cognitive significance. The singular proposition theorists deny the opacity of names and indexicals and provide reasons for doing so that they and many others, including me, find compelling. But they can't plausibly deny that the assertion of different sentences that would express the same singular proposition can have different cognitive significance – that is, that a competent speaker could regard one as true but not so regard the other.

We do many things when we utter a sentence in addition to expressing a proposition, and what we can do differs among sentences that express the same singular proposition. Suppose we are talking, and someone is walking towards us clearly intending to join our conversation. I suspect you don't recognize her and say, "Debra Satz is going to join our conversation." I intend for you to learn her name. If I say, using the description referentially, "The person walking towards us is going to join our conversation," I will have expressed the same singular proposition, but in a way that does not enable you to learn her name. If I say, "The new dean of Humanities and Sciences is going to join our conversation," even if I use the description referentially I will manage to convey something important that I wouldn't convey with "Debra Satz is joining our conversation."

On Frege's view, I would accomplish these different things by expressing different propositions. But the advocate of singular propositions can't say this. The natural thing is to say that I accomplished these things in virtue of *the way* I expressed the proposition. The singular propositonalist has to distinguish between *what* is expressed reported in indirect discourse, and *how* it is expressed reported in direct discourse. He has to appeal to *how* things are expressed for cases the Fregean explains in terms of *what* is expressed. To get at the how, we need to consider how sentences end up expressing the contents they do. Part of this will be understanding how indexicals and names manage to refer to the objects to which they refer and contribute to the content – that is, the singular proposition expressed. (I'll occasionally consider descriptions used referentially, but mostly stick to indexicals and names.)

3   Characters and Modes of Presentation

Cappelen and Dever say something rather surprising about Kaplan's theory:

> The basic Kaplanian framework makes use of a very coarse-grained notion of content: contents as functions from worlds to truth-values. But a central insight of the framework – the isolation of context sensitivity into a character level of meaning – can be preserved even if one prefers a different theory of content. Characters can just as well be functions from contexts to structured propositions, *or from contexts to Fregean thoughts*. What persists across such variations is that the

implementation of context sensitivity resides entirely in character, not in content. [My italics] (p. 16)

In his formal theory in "The Logic of Demonstratives" and "Demonstratives," Kaplan works within possible world semantics. He takes propositions to be sets of world/time pairs; I've been ignoring times and will pretty much continue to do so. The worlds are conceived as having overlapping domains of objects, so objects in the actual world also occur in other possible worlds. The singular proposition which I expressed with "I am making a mess" was the set of worlds in which JP, one and the same person, is making a mess.[12] In a number of places, Kaplan emphasizes that more structured conceptions of propositions, perhaps as basically sequences of relations and objects, would do as well, and might be more intuitive. But whether sets of worlds, or sequences of relations and objects, these are *singular* propositions. They have objects as constituents. He never suggests that Fregean Thoughts could be the contents we get to from character and context.

But why couldn't they be? Consider my utterance of "I am making a mess." Set times and worlds aside for now. To get to a singular proposition, we need the property of making a mess. Once we have that, all we need for a Fregean Thought is a sense that determines me as referent. But don't the character and context give us what we need? Can't the character plus content produce a Fregean sense? Kaplan's theory provides a condition of reference. What we need for Fregean senses are the conditions of reference. So don't we have what we need?

An example where the referent is not an element of context will be helpful. I'll use a further variation on Cappelen and Dever's Fregean Counterpart of my shopper case, where it is not Superman but an ordinary-looking fellow who doesn't resemble Clark Kent who is making the mess. I let go of the cart and seem about to walk off. "What are you doing?" Lois asks. "That man is making a mess," I reply, looking in the direction of a nondescript man. "And so?" she

---

12. David Lewis had quite a different view of possible worlds, in which individuals are "world-bound." See Saul Kripke, *Naming and Necessity* (1980), 42ff for an explanation of the difference and an argument in favor of the view he and Kaplan share on this issue.

asks. "I'm going to tell him to clean it up," I reply. It seems clear that in some sense I have a "mode of presentation" of the nondescript man that I could express with "the man I am looking at." Lois will follow my gaze, see the man, and acquire a mode of presentation as the man she is looking at, or, as she might put it, "the man you are looking at and I am now looking at, too."

But neither of us have expressed a Fregean mode of presentation of the nondescript man, the sort required to yield a Fregean Thought. We have expressed what I will call a *singular mode of presentation*, which picks out a particular man given, in the first case, that I am the speaker or agent, and in Lois's case, that she is talking to me.

It seems that in Kaplan's theory, indexicals *almost* provide Fregean senses. If Castañeda is right, and the two really essential indexicals are 'I' and 'now', we can say that Kaplan's theory provides Fregean senses for indexicals *given* senses for 'I' and 'now'.

This is, I think, quite relevant to the challenge before us. Consider "tomorrow." Simply in virtue of its character – that is, its meaning – it provides a way of referring to or thinking of a day in virtue of the relation it has to us at the moment of speech or thought. If on October 4 I say, "I'm flying to Omaha tomorrow," I am referring to October 5 in this way, *via* the function, the character, associated with the word. If I refer to October 5 in this way, it seems that I must be thinking of October 5 in this way, however else I may also be thinking of it. If on the other hand I simply say on October 4, "I am flying to Omaha October 5," replacing the indexical "tomorrow" with the date, "October 5," the cognitive significance of my remark changes. I express the same singular proposition, but in a different way, that does not require that I am thinking of October 5 as "tomorrow." The difference might be important. If my wife, fearing I will not get ready, says, "You remember that you are flying to Omaha" and I reply, "Yes, I'm flying to Omaha tomorrow" her fears may be allayed. But not if I say "Yes, I'm flying to Omaha October 5." Although she hasn't read Frege or Kaplan, she realizes that I may regard "I'm flying to Omaha October 5" as true, while not regarding "I'm flying to Omaha tomorrow" as true. The effect of the substitution on cognitive significance seems directly connected to the meaning of the indexical substituted for.

So, in Kaplan's new referentialist, singular propositionalist account of indexicals and demonstratives, characters seem to at least partly explain differences in cognitive significance. Intuitively, they correspond to modes of presentation, *almost* providing Fregean senses. Perhaps this accounts for Cappelen and Dever's view that Fregean Thoughts could serve as Kaplan's contents.

4   The Cognitive Significance of Proper Names

The term "direct reference" is now commonly used to describe the views of Donnellan, Kripke, Kaplan, and other new theorists of reference about proper names. It is potentially misleading.

The dominant view, or family of views, is that there is some causal (or historical, or informational, or all three) chain of events that connects a proper name, or a use of a proper name, to events involving the person or object to which it refers. I like the view, especially my version of it in *Reference and Reflexivity* (2011, II). But in any version, why is this *direct*? When I use the name "Aristotle," I manage to refer to a person who lived many centuries ago. The chain that makes it the case that I refer to the ancient logician presumably started with Aristotle's parents, and then continued through events of Greeks talking and writing, Aristotle's manuscripts being lost and then rediscovered, these manuscripts and what his contemporaries said about him being discussed, stored in libraries, translated from Greek to Arabic to Latin and eventually to English. Will Durant used 'Aristotle' in *The Story of Philosophy* (1961); I read the book and learned the name. The chain involves names in different languages that aren't spelled like the English 'Aristotle' and are pronounced differently. That all doesn't seem very direct.

What advocates of "direct reference" theories of names are getting at is not that there is an unmediated connection between names and their referents, but that the mediation isn't of the sort Frege had in mind. They are direct in the sense that a Fregean sense does not mediate the connection. But is it even completely obvious that this is so? Can't we regard the causal theory as an *instance* of Frege's account?

At a rather high level of generality, we can say that Frege thought that proper names were associated with conditions, by the conventions and practices of language, and the referent is whatever object uniquely meets those conditions. In the causal theory, my use of 'Aristotle' seems more or or less directly associated, because of how proper names work in natural languages, with the condition of being the origin of a particular causal chain, the one that stretches from my use back through Durant's book and his sources and eventually to Aristotle's parents. And it seems indirectly associated with Aristotle, because he meets the condition of being the origin of the chain, the person they dubbed 'Αριστοτελης.'

But this is to ignore a good part of what Frege had in mind with senses. As we saw, senses of names are supposed to capture cognitive significance, roughly the criterial beliefs about the referent that the people who use the name have about the referent. Regarding a sentence containing a proper name as true involves thinking that the referent fits the sense; this is something a sincere speaker who uses the name should believe if she regards the sentence in which the name occurs as true. The condition of being the origin of the causal chain is not part of the cognitive significance of names, in this sense – at least for most of us most of the time. Suppose, for example, that Frege at some point said, "Aristotle was a great logician." Can we infer that Frege believed that Aristotle was the origin of the causal chain that led to his use? It doesn't seem we can.[13] He might well have believed it if he had thought about it. But it doesn't get at the criteria he associated with the name. So, while the causal theory may not seem very direct, in the ordinary sense, it does seem distinctly non-Fregean. It suggests

---

13. Since I think the causal chain theory explains how names work, I think anyone who knows how to use names is *attuned* to it. So Frege was attuned to it, and John Searle is attuned to it. But attunement doesn't require belief, except in a very broad sense.

a quite different picture of how proper names work, one which sees them working in a very different way than indexicals.

Frege distinguishes between "perfect" languages, in which all speakers are required to associate the same senses with names, and imperfect languages, like all natural languages, in which differences are "tolerated" (Frege 1960b, 58n). Why do names, in ordinary "imperfect" languages, have cognitive significance at all? Many say that proper names don't have *meanings* in the same sense that other part of speech do. Names occur in encyclopedias but not dictionaries. If this is right, proper names don't acquire their cognitive significance from their meanings, at least not in the sense that you can find the meanings of words in dictionaries.

Examples from Kripke, Donnellan, and others suggest that we don't have to believe very much that is true about the referent of the name we use in order to successfully refer. It seems that if someone uses the name "Aristotle," the most we can infer is that they think that by doing so they are (or at last may be) referring to someone that at least some people call by that name. An inattentive student says after a lecture on classical philosophy, "Aristotle wrote *The Republic* and some other dialogues about Socrates." She has said something false about Aristotle.

Suppose I come upon a conversation where interesting things are being said using the name "Sandy." I am intrigued. I want to join the conversation and learn more about Sandy. I ask, "Is Sandy Orphan Annie's dog or the great Dodgers' pitcher?" I refer to, and ask a question about, whichever Sandy they are talking about. The only belief associated with my use of "Sandy" was that the person or dog or object or event I thereby referred to was being called "Sandy." The causal account of names justifies this belief. But I don't need to believe in that account to form the belief. Doing so is simply a matter of knowing how we use names. So it seems that in the causal, "direct reference" account of names, names have a rather thin cognitive significance, one that doesn't fit Frege's theory very well.

5   The Cognitive Significance of Indexicals

Now compare this with Kaplan's theory of indexicals. Indexicals have (non-constant) characters associated with them by the conventions of particular languages. Characters are *meanings*. You can look them up in dictionaries. You don't learn "I" or "you" or "here" or "now" by encountering it in *The Story of Philosophy* or a casual conversation and then simply using the same expression to refer to the same thing. You have to grasp its character, the relations between uses of the indexical and the person, time, place, or whatever to which that use of it refers. Indexicals are, in this respect, quite unlike names. As I said above, they *almost* give us Fregean senses. They give us singular modes of presentation.

Kaplan calls indexicals "devices of direct reference." Misleading, I think, but he is quite clear about what he means. It's not that that there is a direct, unmediated link between uses of indexicals and what they refer to. In his theory, the route from use to reference is mediated by character and context. Nor is it that they do not supply cognitive significance. A person who uses "I" is thinking of the referent as himself or herself. A person who uses "you" is thinking of the referent as the person to whom they are speaking.

Indexicals are directly referential, in Kaplan's sense, because they *directly* contribute their referent to the proposition expressed by the sentences in which they occur. They don't contribute a Fregean sense, which then determines a reference for the proposition to be about. This is a slightly different sense of "direct" than that involved in calling proper names "directly referential." But the end result is the same: Fregean senses are not involved, and the content of the assertion is a singular proposition. Whether a name or an indexical, the conditions of reference are not incorporated into *what* is said, and cognitive significance is lost at the level of content.

6   Comparing Indexicals and Proper Names

I suggested above that what Cappelen and Dever were really getting at, in their Chapter 3 discussion, were these principles:

Indexicals and Cognitive Significance.
Substituting indexicals with co-referential expressions may change the cognitive significance of the sentences in which they occur, including their explanatory force.

Referring Expressions and Cognitive Significance. Substituting any referring expressions with co-referential expressions may change the cognitive significance of the sentences in which they occur, including their explanatory force.

Given these reasonable principles, they pose the challenge of finding anything special about indexicals as opposed to referring expressions in general, with respect to changes in cognitive significance resulting from such substitutions, especially changes relevant in explanatory situations. They seem to think that the fact that the first principle is a special case of the second, which also applies to names, suggests that there are no important differences. I can't see why it would suggest this. Humans and lizards are animals. The principle that humans need nutrition is a special case of the principle that animals need nutrition. But there are interesting differences between humans and lizards which explain, for example the different ways we treat bugs. As we have seen, new theories of reference tell rather different stories about how indexicals refer and proper names refer. Would it be so surprising to find, in these differences, something of interest about indexicals and explanatory force that didn't apply to names?

The story about Superman and me in the supermarket is what Cappelen and Dever call a "Fregean Counterpart" to the stories I tell in "The Problem of the Essential Indexical" and other such stories. The Fregean Counterparts differ from the originals in that they do not contain indexicals. Substitution of names for names leads to changes in cognitive significance in line with the second principle, but the first is not involved. Here is the whole counterpart:

Pushing my cart down the aisle I was looking for CK (Clark Kent) to tell him he was making a mess. I kept passing by Superman, but couldn't find CK. Finally, I realized, Superman was CK. I believed at the outset that CK was making a mess. And I was right. But I didn't believe that Superman was making a mess. That seems to be something that I came to believe. And when I came to believe that, I stopped looking around and I told Superman to clean up after himself. My change in beliefs seems to explain my change in behavior. (p. 61)

Unfortunately, Cappelen and Dever do not tell us what what problem this case presents for anything I actually claimed. As Arthur Falk points out, there are clear disanalogies:

> One indication of disanalogy between Perry's cases and the 'Frege puzzles' [Cappelen and Dever] devise is the symmetry or duality of their cases and the lack of symmetry or duality in Perry's. Present their thought experiment with the names interchanged, and it will have no effect on the intuitions generated. This is easily shown for their Superman/Kent case. But tell the messy shopper story with 'I' and 'the shopper with the torn sack' or 'the person who was here before' interchanged, and the story becomes nonsensical. Thus no such symmetry or duality exists in Perry's thought experiment. … The situation is similarly symmetrical for their reworkings of the lost hiker and amnesiac Lingens cases (pp. 62f), but not for the cases in their original form. The asymmetry of the original cases is symptomatic of an underlying metaphysical reality, the foundational mental states. Their own cases lack this symptom. (Falk 2015, p. 12)

Explanations in general occur in contexts in which a lot is taken for granted, and what is proffered as an explanation completes the picture in a way that provides something like a sufficient condition for what is explained, or at least a condition that makes what is explained probable, given what is taken for granted. This is certainly the case in my example of the messy shopper, for which this is a Fregean Counterpart. The fact that I acquired the belief I expressed with "I am making a mess" explains my straightening up the torn sack of sugar in my cart on the assumption that I feel responsible for my messes and a lot more. All of these things are natural to assume, given the way I described that case.

In the Fregean Counterpart, we are told that in the beginning I believe that Clark Kent is making a mess. I come to believe that Clark Kent is Superman, and infer that Superman is making a mess. This explains my telling Superman to clean up after himself, but only given many assumptions naturally suggested by the description of the case. For one thing, I have to recognize Superman. Suppose while I am looking for Clark Kent I take a break and read a Superman comic. I realize that Clark Kent is Superman. So what? The fact that I pass by Superman doesn't fill in the gap in the explanation without the assumption that I recognize him. If we change the relevant passage to

> I kept passing by Superman, but didn't recognize him ...

there will be no contradiction with the rest of description Cappelen and Dever give of the case. The original passage certainly suggests that I recognize Superman. It suggests it, because without this assumption, the explanation doesn't work. Let's make it explicit:

> I kept passing by Superman, and I recognized him, but couldn't find Clark Kent.

Cappelen and Dever say,

> A Frege counterpart is a case like the original one in all relevant respects except that the substitution failure involves names instead of indexicals.

We can make the parallel closer if we alter my messy shopper case. Suppose, when I figure out what is going on, I don't say, "I am making a mess" but "JP is making a mess!" Or, "I just came to believe that JP is making a mess!" This would probably work fine as an explanation, at least for those who recognized me and knew my name. (I'm not as recognizable as Superman, so this doesn't include most people). They would assume that I knew that I was JP, otherwise it wouldn't be much of an explanation for my straightening the sack in my cart. Similarly, in the Superman case, one assumes the shopper recognizes Superman as the man he has been passing by. Even if he isn't wearing a cape and external underwear, he probably gets inaccessible items on high shelves by leaping at a single bound. So, in both cases, as far as I can see, we do have the same phenomenon. Both explanations involve an implicit assumption of recognition.

Their case is of the sort Frege once found puzzling, in that two sentences with co-referential names have different cognitive significance, and in that sense the case is Fregean. But it is not Fregean in the sense of being a case for which Frege's theory of sense and reference provides an explanation. There is no Fregean Thought that gets at the belief I have in virtue of which I recognize that the shopper I have been passing by is Superman.[14] Let *JP* be a sense for "JP," and *SM* be a sense for "Superman," and *T* a sense that determines the time at which I walk by Superman. Whatever we choose for these senses, the Thought that *JP* walks by *SM* at *T* will be true or false independently of who believes, when, and where. If you have been taking the story unduly literally, you probably believe such a Thought now. Whichever Thought you believe, you won't be motivated to walk up to anyone and tell them to clean up after himself. The Thought, whatever it is, won't by itself explain my doing so in the market.

Singular propositions fare even worse. If I believed the singular proposition that Clark Kent was making a mess at the beginning of the story, I also believed the singular proposition that Superman was making a mess. Anyone at any time in any place who has names for me, Superman, and the relevant time can believe the singular proposition I believe at the end of the story, which won't motivate them to approach anyone and tell him them to clean up the mess he is making any more than the Fregean Thought would.

To get at the explanation for why my acquisition of my belief that I was the shopper with the torn sack in my case, or that Superman was Clark Kent in their case, we need to consider not only *what is believed* but *how it is believed*.

So I agree in part with Cappelen and Dever: my example and theirs lead to the same conclusion. In both cases, to fully understand the explanations given by belief-reports, we need to understand not just what is believed but how it is believed. In both cases, this information is implied, or at least implicated, by using the belief reports as expla-

---

14. I'll qualify this claim in the next chapter.

nations. But, in both cases, the way one would naturally express the beliefs in order to make what is implied or implicated explicit would employ indexicals and demonstratives. So their Fregean Counterpart does nothing to show their thesis, that there is nothing special about indexicals in explanatory contexts.

5

Names and Indexicals: Frege's Theory of Reference

1 Frege on 'Today' and 'Yesterday'

Now I will respond to Cappelen and Dever's challenge, charitably interpreted, from a Fregean perspective. I assume the basic outlines of Frege's account of how proper names refer are familiar. Frege's only extended discussion of indexicals is in "The Thought," and it is not very long. Here is what he says about 'today' and 'yesterday':

> If someone wants to say the same today as he expressed yesterday using the word 'today', he must replace this word with 'yesterday'. Although the Thought is the same its verbal expression must be different so that the sense, which would otherwise be affected by the differing times of utterance, is re-adjusted. The case is the same with words like 'here' and 'there'. In all such cases the mere wording, as it is given in writing, is not the complete expression of the thought, but the knowledge of certain accompanying conditions of utterance, which are used as means of expressing the thought, are needed for its correct apprehension. The pointing of fingers, hand movements, glances may belong here too. The same utterance containing the word 'I' will express different thoughts in the mouths of different men, of which some may be true, others false. (Frege 1956, p. 296)

Suppose I said, on Tuesday, November 5, 2018, "The midterm elections be today." (For simplicity, I speak a dialect of English that omits tense when there are temporal indexicals in the sentence.) If I had repeated this sentence on Wednesday, my utterance would have been false. One is *required* to substitute for the indexical "today" in order to avoid changing the truth-value of the sentence. If I substitute "yesterday", the resulting sentence will be true, uttered on Wednesday.

Frege here anticipates Kaplan in an important way. The conventional meaning of "The midterm elections be today" and "The midterms elections be yesterday" do not, by themselves, determine propositions. One has to take an "accompanying condition of utterance" into account – in this case, the time of utterance. This is, clearly, not something we are required to do with proper names, including dates, which on Frege's usage would be counted as names.

But of course there is an important difference. In Kaplan's account, the proposition expressed by uttering "The midterm elections be today" on Tuesday and also by uttering "The midterm elections be yesterday" on Wednesday is a singular proposition with November 5 as a constituent. November 5 is the day during which my Tuesday utterance occurred, and so, given the character of "today" and the time of utterance, we have what is required for this proposition. The different character of "yesterday" "adjusts" for the difference in context of my Wednesday utterance, yielding the result that both utterances express the same singular proposition. All we need from the context or "accompanying conditions of utterance" is the time.

But for Frege, the proposition that is expressed by the different utterances is not a singular proposition but a Thought. It seems that we need to supplement what the sentences give us in virtue of their meanings, not only with the time of the utterance, but also with a sense (or something closely related to a sense) that can combine with the meanings of "today" and "yesterday." We need to arrive at a sense that determines November 5 as referent. In addition, the resulting sense or senses have to combine with "the midterms elections be" to give us the same Thought.

On Tuesday, November 5, 2018 at 10 a.m. when I say "The midterm elections be today," I express a true Thought. Language gives us the meanings of "The midterm elections be" and "today". The first phrase seems to have a sense that without any supplementation determines a certain property that various days have. But "today" does not completely determine a sense that determines November 5 as referent. Some supplementation is required. This is supplied by the "accompanying condition of utterance". The relevant condition seems to be the time of utterance, 10 a.m. November 5. But exactly how does this time supplement the meaning of "today" so that we arrive at a sense that refers to November 5? It seems that on Frege's theory we need not just the time, but a sense that determines the time as referent. We seem to need what in "Frege on Demonstratives" I called a "sense-completer." Finding such sense-completers is a problem.

Now consider the relation between Tuesday's utterance of "The midterm elections be today" and Wednesday's utterance of the same sentence. The same sentence expresses different Thoughts on the two days. If we assume that the contributions of "The midterm elections be" and "today" are the same on both days, the difference in Thoughts must derive from the sense-completers, or in some other way Frege hasn't explained. On November 5 we need a sense-completer that combines with the meaning of "today" to determine November 5 as reference and provide the true Thought. On November 6 we need one that combines with the meaning of "today" to determine November 6 as reference and thus express a false Thought.

Suppose on November 5 I have a belief I would express with "The midterm elections be today", and Lois has a belief she would express with those words on November 6. My belief is true; hers is false. But we would both be motivated to go to the polls and vote on the day of the belief – I would succeed in voting, she would not. It seems to be a type A case: believing different things, but in the same way.

Now consider the relation between the two true utterances, of "The midterm elections be today" on Tuesday and "The midterm elections be yesterday" on Wednesday. Frege says:

> Although the Thought is the same its verbal expression must be different so that the sense, which would otherwise be affected by the differing times of utterance, is re-adjusted.

But should the Thought be the same? The belief expressed by

"The midterm elections be today" on Tuesday motivates responsible citizens to go to the polls. The belief expressed by "The midterm elections be yesterday" on Wednesday will not motivate responsible voters to go to the polls. It seems the cognitive significance of the beliefs are different. It seems to be a type B case: different believers believe the same thing in different ways.

It seems that something like the following principle holds. Someone who regards the sentence "the midterm elections be today" as true, and desires to cast a vote, will have a reason to go to the polling place on the day he regards it as true. This holds for both Lois and me, although the belief that leads her to regard the sentence as true is false, and mine is true. My action will be successful; hers will not. So there is something connected with the way these beliefs are held that is important in motivation, even though the beliefs involve different Thoughts, one true, one false.

This all seems quite different than the way dates or other names of particular days would work. The belief I need, on November 5 or any other day, to regard "The midterms election be November 5" will be the same Thought on any other day on which I regard the sentence as true. This Thought, by itself, will not motivate much of anything.

2 Frege on 'I'

In the quotation above, Frege does not consider this issue. His subsequent remarks on 'I', however, suggest an approach he might have taken to deal with it. Here I return to the passage that I spent most of my sabbatical year contemplating:

> Now everyone is presented to himself in a particular and primitive way, in which he is presented to no one else. So, when Dr. Lauben thinks that he has been wounded, he will probably take as a basis this primitive way in which he is presented to himself. And only Dr. Lauben himself can grasp Thoughts determined in this way. (298)

As I said, there are two ways to take the first sentence. If it means "There is a particular and primitive way in which each person is presented to himself, and no one else, and in which he is not presented to anyone else" it would express my view. I take this primitive mode of presentation to be a role involved in perception, introspection, prioperception, and interoception, the special ways we have of knowing about our environment, the positions of our limbs, what's going on inside our bodies, and what's going on in our minds. There is a special way, or special ways, of knowing about oneself, and we all use them. And I think something similar is involved in our knowledge of the present moment; there is a special way of being presented with a given time that each of us can use to find out about what is happening at that time – basically perception plus the other things just listed. But we can't use these methods at one time to find out what happens at another time.

However, it's pretty clear from the rest of the passage that Frege had a different order for the quantifiers in mind: "For each person, there is a particular and primitive way in which he is presented to himself and no one else ... and no one else can grasp Thoughts determined in this way." That is, we each have Thoughts about ourselves with a special primitive sense that determines us as reference, and others cannot grasp that sense, or Thoughts with it as a component.

Suppose Dr. Lauben feels hungry. Then, it seems, he will grasp a Thought with his primitive self-sense as a component that is true if and only if he is hungry. He doesn't need to say anything to himself. If he goes to the kitchen to get a sandwich, it seems that the desire that motivates him will have his self-sense as a component. But if he says "I'm hungry" to someone else, he will not convey the same Thought to them. If they realize who is talking to them, they will have a Thought with whatever sense they use to think about Dr. Lauben as a component. They will not be motivated to get something to eat by having this Thought in the way they would if they have a self-Thought that they were hungry.

Frege's account of thoughts about ourselves seems to be a theory of limited accessibilty as described in "The Problem of the Essential Indexical." All Thoughts are true or false, independently of context.

But some senses and so some Thoughts can only be *grasped* by certain people. It seems the theory could be extended to deal with 'now', by positing senses that could only be grasped at certain times. We suppose that there is a special and primitive way that each time is presented to us *at that time* and no other. This primitive sense could combine with the meanings of 'today' to give me a special way of having the Thought I could spell out (more or less) with "The midterm elections be the day in which *now* occurs" at the time I make my utterance. And this is the Thought I express at that time by saying "The midterm elections be today." Similarly for 'yesterday'. It seems these special now-senses could be used to explain the different references of uses of 'today' and 'tomorrow' on different days, while allowing the indexicals to have the same cognitive significance on different days, just as Dr. Lauben thinking to himself, "I am hungry" will lead to the same sort of behavior that the a similar bit of thinking in his neighbor would, although the Thoughts are different.

I have no completely definitive objection to such theories beyond those given in "Frege on Demonstratives," which many found unconvincing. In that essay, I said that I thought this move was out of the spirit of Frege's concept of Thoughts as objective possibilities, available to all, the same for whoever grasps them at any time. Many reputable Frege scholars disagreed with me, but I still think that. But, setting Frege interpretation aside, I think my approach is preferable given a naturalistic take on the way things work, which I more or less assumed there, admittedly not a definitive objection to the view. Norman Kretzmann made the point that theories of limited accessibility are unable to account for God's omniscience (1966), but that's not an objection to which I would appeal.

The theory so far, however, would not quite work for Frege when extended to temporal indexicals. He wants there to be a single Thought that I express on Tuesday with 'today' and on Wednesday with 'yesterday'. But in this proposal, there would seem to be different Thoughts, with different special now-senses inside them. And even if I say "The midterm election be today" at two different times on Tuesday, it seems I wouldn't express quite the same Thought, although one cannot say for sure without a fully spelled out theory of senses and Thoughts.

3 Non-self-substitutabilty

In their interpretation of Frege's remarks about indexicals, Cappelen and Dever take him to be talking about opacity. Frege says nothing about opacity in his discussion. But I think Frege would have clearly recognized that the account of opacity for indexicals and demonstratives needs to have a small additional proviso not required in the case of proper names, for his own theory predicts it. Indexicals and demonstratives are what I call 'non-self-substitutible (NSS for short). We are often *required* to make substitutions to preserve the truth-value of indirect discourse and attitude reports in which they occur. I say on Tuesday, "I believe the midterm elections be today." I can't report this on Wednesday by saying "I believed that the midterm elections be today." At some point Wednesday Lois says, "I believe that I missed my chance to vote." I can't report this by saying, "Lois believes that I missed my chance to vote." This is simply a consequence of the fact that Frege points out, that the reports have different accompanying circumstances which lead to different Thoughts for the same embedded sentences.

4 Conclusion

Both the new theory of reference and Frege's theory treat indexicals and proper names as working in quite different ways that are clearly relevant to issues of cognitive significance and explanatory force.

5 The Missing Theory

At this point, it would be helpful to look at Cappelen and Dever's account of proper names and indexicals to see if it provides any reason to suppose that there are no differences that might be relevant to issues of cognitive significance. They tell us a bit about it. They tell us that it is non-Fregean and is based on insights gleaned from many excellent philosophers whom they list. But in the end, they say:

> It is true that we haven't given (and won't give) you our theory of opacity. If we did that it would a) take a very, very long time – it would in effect be a separate book project, and b) it would make our arguments hostage to the acceptability of that theory. We are convinced that we can address Diagnostic Distinctiveness by showing that the issues that arise are either theory-internal problems for followers of Gottlob Frege, have nothing to do specifically with indexicality, or are trivial corollaries of context sensitivity. Whatever your view of those issues, it will provide no support for the target of this book. (p. 81)

6   Some Boldfaced Hints

Although their own theory is non-Fregean, it seems we should be able to learn something about their approach from their discussion of Frege and the boldfaced principles they reject:

Diagnostic Distinctiveness.   There are reasons for thinking that our account of opacity for e.g. names can't be extended to indexicals.

Fregean Diagnostic Distinctiveness.   Within a Fregean framework, the explanation/theoretical account of opacity for names can't be extended to indexicals.

I take it that these are principles they suppose that I and others taken in by "essential indexicality" advocate, that are rejected on their theory. But since this is based on their confusion of opacity and cognitive significance, it doesn't turn out to be very helpful.

I don't know whether or not I accept the first, since I don't know what their account of opacity is. I don't accept the second principle. As I explained above, indexicals exhibit NSS. But there is every reason to suppose Frege realized this, since the NSS of indexicals is a consequence of his own theory of indexicals. And if he adopts the strategy that seems most promising to deal with cognitive significance, special senses of limited accessibility, or for that matter if he adopts some strategy I didn't think of, his account of opacity won't need to change. Proper names are opaque, because replacing them with other co-referential expressions with different senses does not preserve the indirect reference of the embedded sentence, the Thought. This would also be true for indexicals on the account I suggested for Frege. So, as far as I can see, whatever way he might choose to deal with the cognitive significance of indexicals, he can extend his theory of opacity to them.

What if we charitably suppose that Cappelen and Dever really had the following principles in mind:

Diagnostic Distinctiveness*. There are reasons for thinking that our account of cognitive significance for e.g. names can't be extended to indexicals.

Fregean Diagnostic Distinctiveness*. Within a Fregean framework, the explanation/theoretical account of cognitive significance for names can't be extended to indexicals.

The first seems plausible, but I can't be sure I accept it until I see their account. I do accept the second, but so did Frege. That's the whole point of his discussion of 'today,' 'yesterday,' and 'I.' To repeat, he doesn't mention opacity in his discussion.

Because of the pervasive confusion between opacity and cognitive significance, I can't conclude much about what their theory will look like until they write their book explaining it, so I cannot respond to their challenge within their theory.

6

Referential, Nominal, and Indexical Content

1 Introduction

In later chapters of *The Inessential Indexical*, Cappelen and Dever draw heavily on their concept of *indexical content*. They attribute the concept to Kaplan, Lewis, and me, but none of us used the phrase in the essays they discuss. Kaplan's contents, and mine, are propositions, singular or general, that are true or false independently of context. Lewis simply doesn't use the term 'content' in "Attitudes *De Dicto* and *De Se*." But Cappelen and Dever use the phrase "indexical content" to explain their own views, by contrast with views that appeal to a "revisionary" theory of "indexical content." I don't find the concept very useful in this regard, since I don't know what they mean by it, and they don't spell out the account they take it to revise.

2 Generalizing Content

Later in life, however, I generalized my notion of content and even used the phrase "indexical content." The generalized concept of content simply means 'truth-conditions.' Even later in life, I have pretty much retired 'content' and simply use 'truth-conditions', since 'content' is used in so many ways. In order to meet Cappelen and Dever halfway, so to speak, I'll use 'content' in the sense of truth-conditions and develop concepts of *indexical, nominal,* and *referential* contents of sentences. Then I'll return to Cappelen and Dever's challenge using these concepts.

Referential content is simply what Kaplan calls "content": singular or general propositions that encode *what is said* and *what is believed*.[15]

Return to my 'Sandy' example. Suppose the others are talking about the actress Sandy Dennis, but I don't know which Sandy they are talking about; for all I know, it is Sandy Koufax or even the hurricane Sandy. I say, in order to enter the conversation, or conceal the fact that I have not been paying attention, "Sandy is very interesting." On the easy standards of the new theory of reference, I have managed to refer to Sandy Dennis and expressed the singular proposition that she is very interesting. But this proposition doesn't do a very good job of getting at the beliefs that motivated my remark; it doesn't capture the cognitive significance, the (meagre) reasons that I regard it as true, or at least likely enough to be plausible that it will get me into the conversation.

We can get a better proposition for this purpose if we abstract over the reference of my use of 'Sandy' by existentially generalizing over its actual reference and filling in the conditions for it to refer. Call my utterance **u**.

Referential content of **u**:

- **u** is true IFF Sandy Dennis is very interesting.

Nominal content of **u**:

- **u** is true IFF there is an object to which the utterance of 'Sandy' refers, and that object is very interesting.

All I had to believe in order to regard my remark plausible enough to get me back in the conversation without showing my ignorance

---

15. It won't matter much, but my conception of a proposition is basically Fregean. I start with circumstances, from the *Begriffsschrift*, which I think it was a mistake for him to abandon, and add Thoughts, conceived a bit less devoutly that he seems to have. He took Thoughts to have their truth-values eternally. This may be fair enough for logical truths and necessary truths, but I think ordinary Thoughts are made true or false by what happens in the mental and physical realms. Frege said Thoughts don't change intrinsically but can change extrinsically, as when someone grasps them at a given time. So I conceive of gaining truth-values as an additional sort of external change. Frege could have adopted this view, but at some cost, because it seems to require a three-valued logic. This is spelled out in more detail in *Frege's Detour*.

was that whoever or whatever "Sandy" referred to, since he, she, or it was interesting enough to be the subject of my friends' conversation, perhaps he, she, or it was interesting enough that it would not sound stupid to say "very interesting."

The referential content and the nominal content give different conditions on the right of the 'iff'. But they are consistent, because the referential content is an instantiation of the nominal content, given the additional information that Sandy Dennis is the referent of the utterance of the name "Sandy." When we give necessary and sufficient conditions, there are virtually always some facts assumed; the cited conditions are what else is necessary and sufficient with those facts taken as given. When we move from nominal content to referential content, we are adding a fact of reference to what is given.

Recall the distinction between what Fred discloses and Fred expresses when he says "Cicero was an orator." What he expresses, in the singular propositions view, is the same as he would have expressed with "Tully was an orator." But he would disclose different things, which comes out in the difference in nominal contents, one involving 'Tully', the other involving 'Cicero.'

Indexical content is based on the same idea, except that we take into account the character of the indexical used in formulating the condition of reference. Consider the lost hiker's utterance **u** of "That lake is Lake Gilmore." The referential content is simply that Lake Gilmore is Lake Gilmore. The indexical content is:

> **u** is true IFF there is an object that the speaker of **u** demonstrates and that object is Lake Gilmore.

The indexical content of **u** leaves a lot open, since one can demonstrate objects in pictures and the like. But it does a better job than the referential content of getting at the truth-conditions of belief that motivates the remark in a way that explains why that belief resulted in his change of behavior.

Similarly, the indexical content of the tardy professor's utterance is that there is a time when the meeting starts, and it is the time of the utterance. The indexical content of the messy shopper's remark is that someone is making a mess, and that person is the speaker.

The nominal and indexical contents are also useful in cases in which a hearer doesn't recognize a name, or doesn't know the facts about the context in which an indexical is used. If someone knocks on the door and says, "I'm here," all I really know is that the speaker of the utterance I heard is outside my door.

I should emphasize that indexical and nominal contents are not new candidates for *what* is said. They are semantic properties of utterances that are useful in characterizing the beliefs disclosed on the part of the speaker, and often what a hearer learns from them. The concepts could be adapted to a Fregean theory by using his account of the conditions of reference of names and indexicals it provides.

3   Back to Substitutions

Let's look at Cappelen and Dever's challenge, charitably interpreted, with these concepts. The question is whether substitution of names for indexicals is interestingly different, in a way that has implications for cognitive significance, than the substitution of names for names that occur in their "Fregean Counterparts."

Superman is at the store, neither wearing a cape and external underwear nor dressed as a mild-mannered reporter, but instead face-camouflaging sunglasses, a straw hat, and bib overalls. He has a torn sack of sugar in his cart and is making a mess but doesn't seem to care much. Lois doesn't know who is making the mess. She approaches him and asks, "Do you know who is making the mess?" In the first case, he says "Clark Kent is making the mess." In the second case, he says "Superman is making a mess." In the third case, he says, "I am making a mess."

The change from 'Clark Kent' to 'Superman' will clearly make a difference to Lois. In the first case, she'll go off looking for someone dressed as a mild-mannered reporter to give him a stern lecture about making a mess. In the second, she will go off, with some trepidation, looking for someone in a cape, to timidly ask him if he is aware that he is making a mess, and, since he is probably preoccupied with fighting crime, would he mind if she straightened up his sack of sugar? The two sentences have different cognitive significance for Lois; that is, the beliefs that lead her to regard the sentences as true, and the implications of those beliefs, will be dramatically different. But not much of this is accounted for simply by the change in nominal content between the two remarks. The change in nominal content would be the same for someone who had never heard of Superman or Clark Kent, and would not make much difference on its own. In Lois's case, the change is due to what she already believes about the person called 'Clark Kent' and the person called 'Superman'.

In the third case, there will also be a dramatic difference. Perhaps Lois will say something like, "Well, I don't know how things are in the hick town you probably come from, but here in Metropolis we clean up after ourselves." Here the change is explained by the indexical content of Superman's remark, not prior beliefs Lois has about the man she sees before her in bib overalls. She has many prior beliefs *about* that man, all the beliefs she has about Superman and Clark Kent. But they are no more relevant to what she does than the beliefs she had about the referent of 'Superman' were to what she did when he replied to her question with "Clark Kent."

This seems to confirm that there is an interesting difference between substituting names for names and substituting names for indexicals – one that is relevant to cognitive significance and potentially explanatory force. And, just for the record, none of these cases involve opacity.

4   When Names Explain More

Your phone rings. You pick it up and ask, "Who is this?" Three cases. First case, the caller says, "It's me." Second case, the caller says, "It's Joe Smith," where "Joe Smith" is the name of a friend. Third case, the caller says, "It's Pamela Jones," where you don't know anyone by that name.

The first case will be annoying, unless you can recognize the speaker's voice. It doesn't give you any helpful information for continuing the conversation. Here I might say that the name is *essential* for continuing the conversation, if I weren't worried about provoking free association. At any rate, it's a helpful and useful response. In the second case, you obtain some idea what the call might be about, based on earlier interactions with Joe Smith. In the third case, my reasoning would go something like this: "I don't know anyone by that name. If she were calling from the Clinic or the Dean's Office or some place like that, she would have taken the opportunity to say so. So she's probably calling to sell me new air ducts or try to get me to change to a new credit card." At this point, her name would be useful, in allowing me to hang up politely: "I'm sorry Pamela, I'm busy now" or, depending on my mood, "I'm sorry Pamela, the residents of this house are all dead. I'm the undertaker."

The point is that indexicals aren't always more helpful than names. "What lake are we looking at?" "That lake." Not helpful. "Lake Gilmore." Quite helpful. And sometimes names are important for the explanatory force of a remark. "Why are you changing the channel?" "Donald Trump is giving a speech." Perfectly understandable explanation. "That man is giving a speech." Not as direct; you have took look at the television to see who is speaking.

Korta and I discuss another type of example in *Critical Pragmatics*. Bob Dole is at a dinner party. He tastes his steak and decides it needs more salt. He says, "Please pass me the salt." That's fine. He says, "Please pass Bob Dole the salt." That's pompous. The reason is that the first provides all the information one needs in order to pass the salt to the person who needs it. You are all at the same table, you see and hear who the speaker is; he is sitting in a certain place; you pass the salt in that direction. The second puts a pointless cognitive demand on you; you have to know who Bob Dole is. If you don't, you won't know which way to pass the salt. And even if you do, it sounds pompous; he is assuming everyone knows who he is.

All of these examples show that indexicals and proper names make interestingly different contributions to cognitive significance that may be relevant to explanatory force and many other things – differences explained by nominal and indexical content.

Is this philosophically deep? I have no idea. That's not one of my areas of specialization. One of my teachers, O.K. Bouwsma, said that a point of philosophy was to "quicken the sense of the queer." This was in the sixties, so the default meaning for "queer" was "puzzling." Bouwsma thought that good philosophy required being puzzled by the commonplace. Now there seems to be a new wave in philosophy, which I call "debunking." The talent lies in *not* being puzzled by things that have puzzled many thoughtful philosophers, but instead realizing they are not philosophically deep. I don't have that skill and am too old to acquire it.

7

What About Opacity?

1 Introduction

In this chapter, I'll use "opacity" rather loosely, for the phenomenon that Frege recognized: it seems that substitution of co-referring expressions can change the truth-values of indirect discourse and attitude reports. Frege thought that it seems that way because it is that way; opacity is real. New theorists of reference seem committed to denying that things are as they seem to be. They cannot deny the phenomenon that we are often reluctant to make such substitutions and doing so can make the resulting reports very misleading. But it seems, if they take singular propositions to be the referents of 'that'-clauses, they cannot allow that such substitutions can change the truth-values of the reports.

I have pointed out that I did not discuss opacity in the essays on which Cappelen and Dever focus. But while opacity is not involved in my arguments, it is certainly relevant to the issues I discuss. So, in this chapter, I'll look at some options for new theorists of reference, broadly speaking, with respect to dealing with opacity, that I have held over the years.

2 The Pragmatic Strategy

In *Signs, Language, and Behavior*, Charles W. Morris provided a useful division of the study of language, or "semiotic," that has pretty much been followed in the philosophy of language:

> Pragmatics is that portion of semiotic which deals with the origin, uses and effects of signs within the behavior in which they occur; semantics deals with the signification of signs in all modes of signifying; syntactics deals with combinations of signs without regard for their specific significations or their relation to the behavior in which they occur (Morris 1946, p. 219).

The semantics/pragmatics distinction has sometimes been seen as coinciding with the distinction between types of expressions, and tokens of these types. For a time, indexicals and demonstratives were seen as falling on the pragmatics side of the divide; Richard Montague, for example, called his investigation into the semantics of indexicals "pragmatics." But more commonly, especially since Kaplan's work, the study of the reference and truth of indexicals and sentences that contain them has been regarded as semantics. Kaplan gives us a semantics for types of expressions without reference to tokens or utterances by bringing in contexts as a parameter of reference and truth. In applying his theory, we take the contexts to be provided by utterances, but the resulting conditions on reference and truth of utterances is usually seen as part of semantics. On this usage, pragmatics deals with how we use expressions, given their semantics. That's the way I will use "pragmatics."

One approach to the appearance of opacity for the new theorist of reference is to regard it as a *reluctance* to make substitutions because they are misleading. In *Situations and Attitudes*, Jon Barwise and I adopted this approach. In our account, the attitudes involved sets of situations rather than singular propositions, but we were committed to substitution of names and pronouns preserving truth of the report. We said,

> In general, it seems to us that reluctance to substitute does not have a simple semantic explanation. It isn't simply a matter of the *type* of expression involved, but also the sort of *use* that is being made of the attitude report. In particular applications of the principle of substitution ... are extremely misleading when the following three conditions are all met:
>
> • the resulting attitude report is being used to explain or predict behavior;

- the agent of the attitude has two different concepts of the subject of the attitude ... and
- the difference in concepts is relevant to the behavior to be predicted or explained.

(Barwise and Perry 1999, p. 199)

So if Jonny, facing a Roman History exam, says "Cicero was an orator," it would be misleading to reassure his mother on the basis of this reasoning. "He said that Tully was a Roman orator; so he must believe Tully was a Roman orator; so if 'True or False: Tully was a Roman orator' appears on the exam, he will get it right."

The inadequacy of our theory was quickly pointed about by Scott Soames (1985) and Mark Richard (1983). Suppose Jonny also volunteers, "Tully was not a Roman orator." Can't we reason:

a)   Jonny believes that Cicero was a Roman orator;

b)   Jonny believes that Cicero was not a Roman orator;

c)   Jonny believes that Cicero was a Roman orator and Jonny believes that Cicero was not a Roman orator;

d)   Jonny believes that Cicero was a Roman orator and that Cicero was not a Roman orator;

e)   Jonny believes that Cicero was a Roman orator and was not a Roman orator;

f)   Jonny believes that there is someone who was a Roman orator and was not a Roman orator.

Nothing in our account blocks this train of reasoning. But f) is not just misleading; it is false.

3   The Crimmins Approach

Mark Crimmins and I provided a better account in our "The Prince and the Phone Booth" (Chapter 12 of *The Problem of the Essential Indexical*). It was basically Crimmins's idea, which he developed further in *Talk About Beliefs* (1992), so I'll name the approach after him. I had developed the concept of "unarticulated constituents" for another purpose; he pointed out that it could be used to bring facts about *how* a belief is held into the semantics of belief reports. He had to overcome a good deal of initial skepticism on my part. Up until then, I had been reluctant to actually talk about ideas, preferring less direct ways of describing episodes of belief, like "accepting sentences." Crimmins made me see this was really a prejudice left over from years of worshipping Wittgenstein and Quine and didn't reflect what way I really thought about things. If we regard ideas as important components of beliefs, we can treat them as unarticulated constituents of belief reports.

Our standard ways of reporting things systematically leave important parameters "unarticulated." This may be because they aren't or weren't known about. "It's nine o'clock," with no reference to *where* it is nine o'clock, worked fine for a long time, before the relativity of time of day to location was relevant to conducting one's life. It still works fine for children and for the rest of us most of the time.

Language has ways of articulating such parameters when they become important. Once we had trains that traveled fast enough to make the relativity of time of day to location relevant, so that travelers had to reset their watches, it was easy to start saying things like "It's noon here, so it must be about fifteen minutes later in Reno." Then timezones were standardized, and telegraphs, radio and television were invented, so "It's noon Pacific Standard Time" is now a standard form.

In the case of reporting beliefs and other attitudes, we have, or can introduce, ways of articulating usually unarticulated parameters. Crimmins and I use "via". Jonny has two different ideas, or notions, of Cicero, which govern his use of the 'Cicero' and 'Tully'. He believes, via his 'Cicero' notion, that Cicero was an orator. He believes, via his 'Tully' notion, that Cicero was not an orator. But he has no notion via which he believes that Cicero was an orator and Cicero was not an orator. That is, he has no belief for which the 'that' clauses in e) and f) provide truth-conditions.

So does Jonny believe that Cicero was a Roman orator or doesn't he? The right answer seems to be that he believes that Cicero was a Roman orator and also believes Cicero was not a Roman orator. But we cannot conclude from the latter that he didn't believe that Cicero was a Roman orator. To go from X believing that anything is *not* F, to X *not* believing that the thing is F is usually a reasonable inference. But not when the believer has two notions of the subject of the belief, and no belief whose truth requires that they are notions of the same thing.

This last last point can be made clearer if we adapt concept of nominal content from the last chapter to ideas and beliefs. The referential contents of Jonny's beliefs – that is, what is required for their truth given the facts of reference of the component ideas – are misleading when we are asking about what it would be rational for him to infer from his beliefs. He believes that Cicero was Cicero. He believes that Cicero was Tully. How can he believe that Cicero was an orator and Tully was not? Nominal contents, where we don't take the references of his Cicero and Tully notions as given, don't license the inference. It can be true that there is someone Jonny's Cicero notion is of, and someone his Tully notion is of, and the first was an orator, and the second wasn't. In assessing a person's rationality, we need to look to nominal and indexical contents rather than referential contents.

4   Quasi-Indication

Contrary to Cappelen and Dever's footnote,[16] I discuss Hector-Neri Castañeda's views in "Castañeda on He and I," the fifth chapter of *The Problem of the Essential Indexical*. I recorded my debt to his ideas and examples, but found difficulties with Castañeda's theory of quasi-indicators.

According to Castañeda, in the report "Elwood believes that he is late for class," we would not ordinarily simply construe the 'he' as a pronoun bound to 'Elwood'. If we did so, the report would

---

16. On page 4: "Both Perry and Lewis acknowledge a debt to Castañeda's work. Neither of them specifies in more detail what part of Castañeda they endorse or were inspired by."

give us no information about *how* the agent (Elwood) was thinking about the subject (Elwood). But, Castañeda argues, we do get such information. We take it that he is thinking of himself first-personally; that is, he would express the belief being reported with "I am late for class." According to Castañeda, the 'he' in our sentence is not the ordinary third person pronoun at all. It is rather the quasi-indicator 'he'; call it 'he*'. It is part of the meaning of 'he*' that the agent is thinking of the subject in the first-person way. The requirement is a matter of semantics, the meaning of 'he*', not simply something strongly suggested on pragmatic grounds. It is a linguistic accident, Castañeda says, that we use 'he' for what are really two different words, the ordinary third-person pronoun and the quasi-indictor. He sometimes takes 'he himself' to be a quasi-indicator, the 'himself' basically serving as the asterisk. But he points out that 'he himself' is not always used as a quasi-indicator.

Similarly, I say, "Elwood left after lunch. He thought his class started then." 'Then' is not simply a pronoun whose reference is fixed as the time Elwood left. It is a quasi-indicator that refers to that time but also requires that Elwood had a thought he would have naturally expressed, with "My class starts now."

I'll use "quasi-indication" for the phenomenon on which Castañeda focussed our attention, as I am using "opacity" for the phenomenon on which Frege focussed our attention. In "Castañeda on He and I," I found a number of difficulties with Castañeda's account of quasi-indication, most of which were linked to the (more or less) Fregean framework within which he worked. (I also provided a rather wonderful fantasy, if I may be immodest, which probably does a better job of explaining my point of view than any straight philosophy I have ever written. As far as I can tell, it has now been ignored by two generations of philosophers.)

But comments on an earlier draft by François Recanati, points Falk made in his essays, and works cited in Chapter 9 of *The Inessential Indexical* have led me to take another look at quasi-indication.

Another motive is my view that Eros Corazza is usually right. He provides a much more thorough discussion of Castañeda's views and a sympathetic development of quasi-indication in *Reflecting the Mind* (Corazza 2004). He focusses on the phenomenon of quasi-indication and separates some of Castañeda's central claims from the Fregean framework in which they were developed. Corazza draws on linguistic theory and other languages to support the robustness of the phenomenon of quasi-indication. One thing that worried me about Castañeda's theory was the odd coincidence of using the same words in English for pronouns and quasi-indicators. But Corazza cites other languages in which the same words do not seem to be used for pronouns and quasi-indicators. So I am exploring whether quasi-indication can be combined with the Crimmins view. This is work in progress. I haven't quite made up my mind.

It seems that we can regard quasi-indication as a case of articulating the often unarticulated. Everyone who knows how people work knows that there is a difference between being in a belief state that would lead one to say "I am so-and-so" and one which would lead one to say "N is so-and-so" where 'N', as it happens, refers to me. At least no one who has read Castañeda's wonderful examples can be in doubt about this. The distinction clearly isn't articulated in reports of the form "X believes that S," where 'that S' is taken to refer to a singular proposition. Crimmins and I would articulate the unarticulated parameter with 'via'. Elwood believes, via his notion of the famous war hero, that he did heroic deeds. But Elwood doesn't believe, via his self-notion, that he did heroic deeds.

Can't we regard quasi-indicators as articulating the relevant parameter? I call Castañeda's war hero 'Elwood'. Elwood was wounded in battle, lost his dog tags, and acquired amnesia, which was never cured. He went on to write a biography of the hero of the battle in which he was injured, never realizing that he was the hero. "Elwood doesn't believe he* did heroic deeds" amounts to "Elwood doesn't believe, via his self-notion, that he did heroic deeds." "He*" amounts to "via the first-person". Similarly, "then*" amounts to "via his 'now'-buffer, where the 'now'-buffer is the constantly changing idea associated with what one is perceiving, interocepting, introspecting, and the like at a given time.

In this view, it seems that I would be claiming that the account of opacity for indexicals is different than that for proper names. On the other hand, we might consider extending Castañeda's idea of quasi-indication to names. For any name N there is a quasi-indicator N*. "Jonny believes that Cicero* was an orator" means "Jonny believes, via his 'Cicero'-notion, that Cicero was an orator. This would imply, given that Cicero is Tully, that Jonny believes that Tully was an orator. But it would not imply that Jonny believes that Tully* was an orator. However, there is not much evidence for such nominal quasi-indicators, as far as I can tell.

8

Hume and Heimson

1 The Two Patterns

Recall the distinction between pattern A and pattern B. In pattern A, different things are done in the same way; in pattern B, the same thing is done in different ways. On the singular propositions view, the cases of differing cognitive significance that inspired Frege to abandon his *Begriffsschrift* theory and develop the theory of sense and reference exhibit pattern B. "Hesperus is a planet" and "Phosphorus is a planet" express the same proposition, that Venus is a planet; they are two ways of saying the same thing.

As I said, if one confines oneself to proper names, pattern A cases tend to be ignored. It seems an accident about proper names that we have nambiguity, inessential to understanding the way proper names work, and so not very interesting from the point of view of semantics.

In the case of indexicals, however, it is the essential feature of how they work, relativity of content to context, that leads to the possibility of saying different things in the same way. The examples I used at the beginning of "The Problem of the Essential Indexical" were Type B cases, since I was focusing on how the same person at the same time might say the same thing in two different ways that had different explanatory force. But every Type B case gives rise to Type A cases: imagine another shopper saying "I am making a mess" or the professor saying "The department meeting starts now" a week later or the hiker, earlier in his trek, momentarily confused, pointing to a different lake and saying "That is Lake Gilmore."

As I said, Type A cases take center stage when I give my solution to the problem posed by my Type B cases:

> Now consider all the good-hearted people who have ever been in a supermarket, noticed sugar on the floor, and been ready to say "I am making a mess." They all have something important in common, something that leads us to expect their next action to be that of looking into their grocery carts in search of the torn sack. Or consider all the responsible professors who have ever uttered "The department meeting is starting now." They too have something important in common; they are in a state that will lead those just down the hall to go to the meeting, those across campus to curse and feel guilty, those on leave to smile. (Perry 1979, p. 17)

This is important because Type A cases don't give rise to belief reports that are, or even seem to be, opaque. I say, "I am making a mess." Lois says, "I am making a mess." Superman says, "I am making a mess." We disagree about who is making the mess. We say different things in the same way. We have three reports: JP said that he was making a mess, Lois said that she was making a mess, Superman said that he was making a mess. All three reports are true. The difference is not the result of substitution of a referring expressed in an embedded sentence that occurs opaquely, or seems to. The difference is due to referring to a different speaker at the beginning of the reports.

2   The Missing Counterparts

This means that there are no "Frege Counterparts" for Type A cases. A Frege Counterpart is a case of opacity involving proper names instead of indexicals. But pattern A cases don't even seem to be cases of opacity or apparent opacity. No substitutions are invoved, except the name of speaker. And the explanatory force is not changed as we go from my utterance of "I am making the mess" to Lois's and to Superman's. The point is that the explanatory force is the same, which, in my account is explained by the fact that the same *way* of believing that motivates all three remarks, in spite of the differences in what is said and what is believed.

Consideration of Type A cases, which it would seem hard to avoid if one reads the last section of "The Problem of the Essential Indexical" with any care, should make it clear that I was not talking about opacity. But when Cappelen and Dever turn to a Type A case, this is not the conclusion they come to.

I used one extended Type A case in "Frege on Demonstratives" which they consider:

> Not all cases that are discussed in the literature on indexicals have obvious Frege counterparts, but those that don't are not about opacity at all and so are not in the business of establishing Motivational Distinctiveness.
>
> *Case 4: Hume in His Study*
>
> Perry says:
>
>> Let us imagine David Hume, alone in his study, on a particular afternoon in 1775, thinking to himself, "I wrote the Treatise." Can anyone else apprehend the thought he apprehended by thinking this? First note that what he thinks is true. So no one could apprehend the same thought, unless they apprehended a true thought. Now suppose Heimson is a bit crazy, and thinks himself to be David Hume. Alone in his study, he says to himself, "I wrote the Treatise." However much his inner life may, at that moment, resemble Hume's on that afternoon in 1775, the fact remains: Hume was right, Heimson is wrong. Heimson cannot think the very same thought to himself that Hume thought to himself, by using the very same sentence (Perry 1977, p. 487).
>
> The reason Heimson cannot use the sentence 'I wrote the Treatise' to think the very same thought that Hume thought by using that sentence is that the referent of 'I' depends on the speaker/thinker. That entirely obvious point is the only one made in this example. (We should note however that the case can be developed in ways that would make a non-trivial point about indexicality. One natural way of doing so is to focus on the different behavioral consequences of Hume and Heimson entertaining the same content. We addressed that distinctiveness claim in Chapter 3 and won't rehearse our arguments against it here.) (Cappelen and Dever 2013, p. 64)

The reason the Hume/Heimson case doesn't have a Fregean Counterpart is simply that it is a Type A case. Hume and Heimson say of two different objects that they have a certain property, being identical with David Hume, using the same sentence with the same character. No opacity, real or apparent, is involved.

I don't know what Cappelen and Dever have in mind by saying one could focus on "the different behavioral consequences of Hume and Heimson entertaining the same content." They *don't* entertain the same content; that's the point. They both say, "I wrote the Treatise." As a result, they grasp different Thoughts (on Frege's view) and believe different singular propositions (in Kaplan's). It is the *sameness* of the *way* they entertain *different* contents that makes the case interesting, beyond the trivial point they got out of it. Hume and Heimson lived in different centuries and presumably had quite different systems of belief or total belief-states. But there is something these systems seem to have in common: they were both in a state that led them to say "I am David Hume" when asked who they were. The same state will probably lead both of them to smile when hearing praise of Hume's writings.

3 The Wrong Conclusion

In the opening passage, Cappelen and Dever draw the wrong conclusion. They argue that since the case does not involve opacity, and so has no "Fregean Counterpart," it is irrelevant to a possible connection between indexicals and motivation. They seemed on the verge of seeing the irrelevance of their arguments. Just a slight change in their argument would have done the trick: the case clearly has to do with indexicals and motivation; it does not involve opacity, so opacity is irrelevant.

The example is clearly relevant to the challenge they pose, to find interesting differences between indexicals and names that seem connected with motivation and explanations of action. Heimson and Hume are semantically competent speakers of English. They both regard the same sentence, with the same meaning, "I am David Hume" as true when spoken by them.

This leads them both to sincerely say, "I am David Hume," one falsely, one truly. The belief state they are both in explains their smiling when they hear Hume praised.

But perhaps I don't understand the concept of "Motivational Distinctness," which is a third boldfaced claim they come up with in this chapter to "clarify" what I was getting at. They introduce it with a rather odd remark about Kaplan.

> ... considerations involving indexicals in opaque contexts could provide arguments for a revised notion of content – it could motivate a theory of content in which indexical contents are distinct in ways other than simply having variable characters (in Kaplan's sense). (p. 58)

In Kaplan's theory, contents do not have characters. Kaplan explains his use of "content" as *what* is said or believed. In his theory, the content of a sentence using an indexical or a proper name is a singular proposition. One cannot retrieve character from content. They don't tell us what the considerations involving indexicals in opaque contexts might be.

Here is the principle:

> **Motivational Distinctiveness.** There are reasons for thinking that indexicals interact with opaque contexts in ways that are unique to indexicals, which can't be replicated for non-indexical expressions.

Frege and I, and I would think anyone else who thinks about it, agree that indexicals exhibit NSS and to this extent "interact with opaque contexts in ways that are unique to indexicals." Frege doesn't need to modify his account of opacity to take account of this. It has nothing to do with any claims I made in "The Problem of the Essential Indexical" or about Hume or Heimson.

So consideration of the boldface claim Cappelen and Dever attribute to me reinforces my view that Cappelen and Dever draw exactly the wrong conclusion from the Hume case. It could well have been the point at which they realized their confusions about opacity and cognitive significance were leading them astray – but it wasn't.

9

A Prior Example

1 Introduction

Cappelen and Dever quote Arthur Prior:

> One says, e.g. "Thank goodness that's over!", and not only is this, when said, quite clear without any date appended, but it says something which it is impossible that any use of a tenseless copula with a date should convey. It certainly doesn't mean the same as, e.g. "Thank goodness the date of the conclusion of that thing is Friday, June 15, 1954," even if it be said then. (Nor, for that matter, does it mean "Thank goodness the conclusion of that thing is contemporaneous with this utterance." Why should anyone thank goodness for that?) (1959, p. 17)

In this short paragraph, Prior anticipated many of the central points I was to make twenty years later. I think he deserves credit for this, not discredit. I'll recast his example in terms of cognitive significance, use 'be' for tenseless 'is', and set things up so we can regard it as a case of substitution changing cognitive significance.

Suppose that, after undergoing a root canal or some other painful episode on June 15, 1954[17], the person who underwent the procedure says at 2 p.m.

- "Thank goodness that episode be over as of now!"

The remark has a different cognitive significance than either of the following would have, uttered by the same person at the same time:

---

17. This was a Tuesday, not a Friday.

- "Thank goodness that episode be over as of 2 p.m. June 15, 1954,"
- "Thank goodness that episode be over as of the time of this utterance."

The first sentence conveys relief on its own, while the second would require some supplementation, perhaps "Today is June 15, 1954." An utterance of the third would, as Prior suggests, be rather weird, outside of a philosophy-of-language seminar on tense and indexicals, and those new to those topics probably wouldn't know how to regard it.

A couple of points.

First, the example doesn't involve opacity. There are no belief-reports in it. No change of truth-values is involved, and in fact it's not clear that truth-values have a role in the example. We might say that the remarks have conditions of sincerity: the speaker must be relieved that the episode is over as of the time referred to.

Second, from the singular propositions point of view, we have a Type B cases; the same singular proposition captures the sincerity conditions in all three cases, at least if we take "the time of this utterance" as an accurate but referential use of the description. From a Fregean point of view, we have three different Thoughts.

Third, from either point of view, the example clearly gives rise to Type A cases with respect to the first sentence. Two different recent sufferers at different times could say "Thank goodness that episode be over as of now," talking about different episodes. They would have used the same sentence, with same meaning, to make remarks with different sincerity conditions.

2 Fregean Counterparts

Cappelen and Dever are interested in whether Prior's example supports one of the boldfaced principles they attribute to me and reject:

> **Motivational Distinctiveness.** There are reasons for thinking that indexicals interact with opaque contexts in ways that are unique to indexicals, which can't be replicated for non-indexical expressions.

I don't think Prior's example is an argument for this principle, since it doesn't involve opacity. Be that as it may, Cappelen and Dever think that whatever force it seems to have will be cleared up with a Fregean Counterpart:

> ... it is easy to reconstruct the Prior case so it has a straight-forward Frege counterpart. Suppose now = time t. Then (1) and (2) get different truth-values, because "now" and "t" aren't intersubstitutable:
>
> 1) I am relieved that the event is over now.
> 2) I am relieved that the event is over at time t.
>
> Put that way, the Frege counterparts are easy to produce:
>
> 3) I am relieved Superman is here.
> 4) I am relieved Clark Kent is here.

This seems unusually irrelevant even by the standards of Fregean Counterparts. The uses of 'am' in 3) and 4) seem to be in the present tense. The Counterpart doesn't have 'now' and 'at time t'. In their version of Prior's example, the substitution of 'at time t' for 'now' seems to change the cognitive significance. What does the substitution of 'Superman' for 'Clark Kent' have to do with that?

The point of Fregean Counterparts is to show that the same phenomena that arise with substitution of indexicals arise with with substitution of names. So shouldn't the Fregean Counterpart simply involve names for the same parameter of the situation that the substituted indexical dealt with? In 1) and 2) we have an agent, 'I', the relation of being relieved, a proposition, identified by 'that'-clauses, and the time of the episode of relief, provided by the present tense. The substitution occurs within the 'that'-clause, identifying the time at which the event is over. We have the possibility of opacity, since being relieved is an attitude towards a proposition. If we assume that the speaker doesn't know that "now = time t" or thinks that this is not so, the substitution would change the truth-value, on Frege's approach, or lead to something very misleading on the singular propositions approach.

So, it seems like a Fregean Counterpart should simply start with a name doing the work that 'now' does in 1) – that is, identifying the time that the event referred to in the 'that'-clause. (Cappelen and Dever don't have 'that'-clauses in 3) and 4) for reasons that are obscure, at least to me.) Let's suppose that it is Christmas 2015. That day has two names in my idiolect, "Christmas$_{15}$" and "Noel$_{15}$". So we start with

5) I am relieved that the event is over by Christmas$_{15}$.

6) I am relieved that the event is over by Noel$_{15}$.

5) and 6) might have different truth-values, if the 'that'-clauses refer to Thoughts. Or they will appear to, if they refer to singular propositions. And the embedded sentences have different cognitive significance.

Now the $64 question: So what? Why would this show that indexicals don't work significantly differently, when it comes to cognitive significance, than proper names do, in ways that are explained by the different ways indexicals and names refer?

Oddly, the Fregean Counterpart that Cappelen and Dever provide seems to make the same point. Suppose the utterance takes place at Grant's Tomb. Consider:

7) I am relieved that Superman is here.

8) I am relieved that Superman is at Grant's Tomb.

9) I am relieved that Superman is at the corner of 122nd St and Riverside Drive.

If we take the description in 9) to be used referentially, the 'that'-clauses refer to the same singular propositions. If we are dealing with Thoughts, we have three different ones and can't take the description referentially. But, either way of looking at it, the cognitive significance of the three embedded sentences differs.

Note the interactions of the two tensed copulas, 'am' and 'is'. Tense is a form of context-sensitivity or indexicality, if we use that term to mean expressions that have varying characters. Because of their characters, the same time is both the time of relief and the time of Superman's presence at the location referred to. The characters constrain the relations between these times, quite independently of the time of utterance; that is, we can easily construct Type A cases. No doubt Superman's arrival at Grant's tomb had often been a source of relief to many New Yorkers over the years.

The same thing happens with 'here'. Its character requires that the place where Superman is the same place where the speaker is at the time that is both the time of relief and the time of Superman's presence there. This connection is eliminated when we go from 7) to 8), but not when we go from 8) to 9), since it isn't there in 8).

The fact that indexicals are governed by characters, not historical chains, or Fregean senses, and so within a given utterance have their references mutually constrained through the common context, is of great importance in communication. Perhaps it's not essential, but it certainly is handy. Substitution of names for indexicals breaks these constraints and certainly is relevant to the kinds of changes in cognitive significance that are produced.

3 What Prior Was Claiming

Just prior to the passage Cappelen and Dever quote, Prior says:

> ... half the time I personally have forgotten what the date is, and have to look it up or ask somebody when I need it for writing cheques, etc.; yet even in this perpetual dateless haze one somehow communicates, one makes oneself understood, and with time-references too. One says, e.g. "Thank goodness that's over!" (Prior 1959, p. 17)

Once we reverse the quantifiers on Frege's formula in "The Thought" and recognize that there are ways that each person is presented to himself and no one else, it seems to me many things fall into place. And it seems the same holds for times. There is a way that we are all presented with what's happening at a time, at that time. And indeed, the ways are pretty much the same. Perception is a way of knowing what is going on at the time of perception; proprioception is a way of knowing if one's legs are crossed at the moment of proprioception. We have what I call normally self-informative ways of knowing what's going on, and they are also normally present-informative. Cases in which a person doesn't know who he is are rare. But Prior reminds us that there is nothing unusual about not knowing what time it is. Of course, it is a more nuanced issue. Most of us most of the time don't know what minute of the day it is; many of us much of the time don't know what hour it is, or even what day it is, and sometimes we don't know what month it is. Rip Van Winkle didn't even know what year it was, but his case was a bit unusual, although for the first few weeks after New Year's Day I often forget which year it is.

But people who have amnesia, and people who have lost track of time, still can find out about themselves or the present time using normally self-informative and present-informative methods. And most of the animal kingdom is pretty much limited to such primitive knowledge, or more cautiously such primitive ways of picking up information. When humans have such knowledge, it is natural to express it with indexicals. But this isn't because God or Mother Nature read "On the Logic of Demonstratives" and used it as a manual for constructing life; I didn't claim this, and I doubt that any of the philosophers taken in by my rhetoric and the arguments I parade did, either. 'I' and 'now' give us ways of referring to ourselves even if we don't know who we are, and more importantly ways of conveying information about ourselves to others without presuming that they know who we are, and ways of referring to the moments we are finding out about without being able to identify them by dates or time of day.

4   Prior and McTaggart

In "Thank Goodness That's Over," Prior is usually seen as arguing for, or at least suggesting an argument for, the reality of McTaggart's A series. The A series orders events in terms of being (more or less distantly) past, present, and (more or less distantly) future. It is contrasted with the B series, which orders times and events in terms of the relations of being earlier than, contemporaneous with, and later than. McTaggart argued that to make sense of the A series, we needed to suppose that the B series left something out – the properties that are the basis of the A series: being past, present, and future. He went on to argue that the B series didn't leave anything out; the A series didn't make sense, and since it was an intrinsic component of our concept of time, time is unreal.

In the present interpretation, Prior is arguing that the B series does leave something out, and we need to see being past, present, and future as properties that events and times have, in addition to standing in the relations of being earlier than, contemporaneous with, and later than. (My discussion is heavily indebted to de Ponte and Korta (2017)).

The basic idea is that after his root canal, Prior has a true belief he would express with "the root canal is over." Being over – that is, being in the past – is a property the root canal didn't have until it had occurred. It is a different belief than he would have expressed, in my dialect, with "The root canal be over by 2 p.m. June 15, 1954." This reports a relation that the root canal has to a date that occurs in the B series, and this belief would have been true if Prior had had it a week or a year earlier. We can't get at the difference between the thoughts without recognizing A properties like *being over*.

If this is correct, then the B series does leave something out. One can think of old fashioned paper calendars as B series representations. I still have one on my refrigerator. If I were better organized, it would contain entries for all the important events for a given month, placed in the proper cells, with the time of day included, and used to order in the notations in each cell from top to bottom. But even if my calendar were that well-organized, it would leave something out. It's of no help in organizing my day, until I know what day it is.

Now we have calendars on our computers which don't seem to leave out this information. When I look at my computer calendar, the date on one of the cells is circled in blue. That's supposed to be the day on which I am looking at the calendar. If I set the date correctly when I bought it, and if I have kept it charged up and avoided other computer catastrophes since then, I can be confident that the date circled in blue can rightly be called "today". It supplies some information my paper calendar doesn't. What's going on?

On the computer side of things, we can think of the blue circle as an indexical with the character of 'today'. The computer isn't doing anything that couldn't have done in principle with the paper calendar. I could have my butler arise early every day and write "today" in bright blue in that day's cell, erasing the notation from the day before – if I had a butler.

On my side of things, I already have what I call "primitive knowledge" about what is happening *today* before looking at my computer, and I have primitive knowledge of what is happening *now* before looking at my watch. I know today is the day whose weather I can see by looking outside. If I have a headache, I know that I have a headache now, and so that I have a headache today. And I know what is required to do things today. Perception of various sorts, including proprioception, interception, visceroception, and the like provide us with information about ourselves and the present time, information about what is happening inside of us and around us at the time the perceptions occur. We put can information provided in this way to good use, for the more or less direct effects of our actions concern the very objects we know about in these primitive ways. If I know via visceroception that I need to visit the restroom, I can get the person whose needs I know about in this way to the bathroom, without knowing what day it is, what time it is, or even what my own name is. And these ways of knowing about things are causally connected to emotions, like the trepidation one has before a root canal and the relief one has afterwards.

Indexicals and demonstratives provide us with ways of referring to the objects we find out about – 'me', 'now', 'today', 'that dog' – but we don't need indexicals or demonstratives or language at all to have primitive knowledge and put it to use. Animals have such knowledge, and effectively put it to use, without indexicals.

But humans have an enormous amount of information available about these objects, and many more, in objective formats, with no indexicals. And we need such information to figure out ways of doing many of the things we do. That's what my paper calendar provides. I see that there is a department meeting on February 1 at noon. But how do I integrate that with my primitive knowledge? I go to my computer, see the blue circle around 'February 1', and make plans to get to the meeting. Indexicals are not needed for primitive knowledge, but they are the interface between objective representations and primitive knowledge.

McTaggart thought that if events and times had properties like being present or being past, that would mean the B series left something out. On the present construal, Prior agrees and draws the conclusion: the B series does leave something out. I think they are both wrong. There is a difference between A series representations and B series representations, but they represent the same things. It is the how, not the what, that differs.

McTaggart's A series and B series are the same series, described and thought about in different ways. To adapt one of his examples, consider all the days from Queen Anne's birth until 2050 represented on a large paper calendar in terms of the earlier-than family of relations. Then go to the representation of the day you are conducting this exercise, and prepare a new chart, labelling each day as "n-days in the before today", "today" or "n-days after today" and order them accordingly on a new large piece of paper. This will yield the same days ordered just as they are in the B series.

The original B series calendar representation could contain the words 'be present', 'be past' and 'be future', assuming, as Prior does, that these are not indexicals, or at least are used "undexically" here in the sense explained in Perry (2017). But it would be redundant. Queen Anne died on August 1, 1714. Our B series representation might include, in the cell for that date, not only "Queen Anne dies" but also "Queen's Anne's death is present" and for the next cell for August 2, "Queen's death is past." But this just means, in the first case, that Queen Anne's death be contemporaneous with the other events in the cell, and, in the second, that it be later than those in the previous cell.

Now there is an oddity here, about which I don't have a settled view. It seems to me in the phrases "the present," "the past," and "the future" the words 'past', 'present', and 'future' have an indexical aspect, and this is exploited in some uses of these phrases. But I won't say more about that here.[18]

The difference between the A series representation of the events and the B series representation isn't in what happens, but in the way the information about what happens is presented. In the A representation it is represented in a way that allows it to be directly integrated with primitive knowledge; in the B representation, it is not. Suppose Fred is inspired to execute the exercise I suggested, on March 1, 2019. He may find in the B representation of that date "Fred translates a B representation of the events since Queen Anne's birth into an A representation." How whoever put together the B representation knew this is a mystery, but its presence in the B representation is not. The B representation doesn't need to leave any fact out. Still, Fred will have to know that he is Fred, and that he only does this once, to learn from this that March 1, 2019 is the day he calls "today" as he carries out the exercise.

Thus I claim that the difference between the A representation and the B representation is not *what* is represented as happening, but *how* it is represented. A representations are useful because we do not have a view on our world from nowhen. B representations are useful because the same representation can be used, unaltered, at different times, to present the same information.

If I am correct, what does this show about the really deep metaphysical issues involved? I think there are some things it shows. And there are even some things, that I am inclined think it does show. But these are issues for discussing at some date later in the B series than today, when my thoughts be more settled.

---

18. For a discussion of relevant issues, see "Indexicals and Undexicals" (2017).

10

Kripke

1 Frege and Kripke's Arguments

Section 4.7 of Cappelen and Dever's book is devoted to objections I made to Frege in "Frege on Demonstratives." The heading is "Perry's Famous Anti-Fregean Arguments Have Nothing Specifically to Do With Indexicality." They continue:

> Perry (1977) argues that indexicals present an obstacle for Fregean theories of meaning and attitude reports. The goal of this section is not to show that Perry's arguments fail, but that they could have been run using names, rather than indexicals. The objections he raises are powerful, but have nothing specifically to do with indexicality. (p. 73)

On Frege's view, sentences, at least those that are complete, express Thoughts, and refer to Thoughts when they are embedded in indirect discourse and attitude reports. Thoughts do not contain objects. What referring terms contribute to the Thoughts expressed by sentences that contain them are senses. As Cappelen and Dever point out, there are many interpretations of Frege. Mine is based on what he says in the 1892 essays where he explained his new theory of sense and reference, and in "The Thought" and two other essays he wrote late in life when he returned to the topic. My interpretation is defended at length in *Frege's Detour*.

On my interpretation, senses (a) contain no objects; (b) provide conditions that will determine a unique object to be the referent, if there is a referent, which there won't be in the case of fictional names and some other cases, such as names introduced as part of faulty

91

theories; (c) explain the difference in cognitive significance between sentences that employ names that refer to the same objects. Frege holds that in "perfect" languages, as he intended his *Begriffsschrift* to be – the book was named for the language – speakers should associate the same senses with the same names. But in imperfect languages, differences in sense can be "tolerated."

> In the case of an actual proper name such as "Aristotle" opinions as to the sense may differ. It might, for instance, be taken to be the following: the pupil of Plato and teacher of Alexander the Great. Anybody who does this will attach another sense to the sentence "Aristotle was born in Stagira" than will a man who takes as the sense of the name: the teacher of Alexander the Great who was born in Stagira. So long as the denotation remains the same, such variations of sense may be tolerated, although they are to be avoided in the theoretical structure of a demonstrative science and ought not to occur in a perfect language (Frege 1960b, 58n).

The two suggested senses for 'Aristotle' are given with definite descriptions which themselves contain names: 'Plato' and 'Alexander the Great' in the first candidate. Plato or Alexander can't be parts of Thoughts any more than Aristotle can, so it seems that the sense must contain senses that determine Plato and Alexander as reference rather than Plato and Alexander themselves. I think it's fair to say Frege doesn't give us a well worked-out theory that explains how this all works. He doesn't have logically proper names in his system as Russell did.

But let's suppose that there is a candidate sense for 'Aristotle' that works the way Frege thought it should and gives us a qualitative sense that picks Aristotle uniquely. It is a *further* question whether this is the way proper names, at least in imperfect languages, actually work. It was this issue that the classic papers by Donnellan and Kripke put into doubt, as I explained in my earlier discussion of names in the new theory of reference.

Cappelen and Dever give three arguments from Kripke, which they call the "Problem of Misdescription," the "Problem of Ignorance," and the "Epistemic Argument."

The first is illustrated by my student who says, "Aristotle is the one who wrote the *Republic*; that's all I know about him." That may express the only belief she has about Aristotle that would have a hope of picking out a unique person – but it picks out Plato instead. Still, she refers to Aristotle and says something false about him. So, even when one has something that is eligible to be a Fregean sense associated with the name, that sense does not determine the reference. Cappelen and Dever say,

> A related problem is sometimes called "the Problem of Ignorance." As Kripke points out, we can use a name, "NN" to refer to NN, without being in possession of any information that uniquely identifies the referent of "NN." (p. 75)

This doesn't seem correct. In the above example, the student could uniquely identify Aristotle as the person she is referring to. As I noted above, on the causal theory of names, there is a condition that the referent of a name uniquely meets when there is referent, being the origin of the causal chain that leads to the use. The student may have no idea about such causal chains. But if she knows how to use proper names, she can be confident that she has referred to whomever the instructor referred to with the name; she is simply extending the chain. She will know that there is someone called "Aristotle" to whom she has referred. But this condition is not what Frege had in mind with senses. I think the problem of ignorance is simply that; one can refer with a name while being abysmally ignorant of the referent – in the case of Sandy, not knowing whether the referent was an actress, a dog, a Dodger, or even a hurricane, and so not coming anywhere close to what Frege had in mind.

They explain the "Epistemic Argument" thusly:

> Suppose the descriptive content I associated with "NN" is "the F." Getting to know the information expressed by "NN is the F" requires work that's not required to come to know that "The F is the F." (p. 75)

The criticism they make of my arguments is not that they are wrong, but:

> For those with even a slight familiarity with the literature, it should be clear that [Perry's] arguments against the Fregean account of

indexical reference are simple instantiations of familiar and general objections to Fregeanism found in Kripke. In particular, they are instantiations of the objections sometimes referred to as the "Problem of Misdescription," the "Problem of Ignorance," and the "Epistemic Argument." (p. 75)

2 An Important Difference

But this is simply to miss some important points. Kripke's arguments don't depend on there *not being* senses of the sort Frege required for names, but on such senses *not being required* to use names. Setting aside the worries above, *being the pupil of Plato and teacher of Alexander the Great* seems to be a sense that determines Aristotle as referent. In a philosophy-of-language course devoted to Frege's footnote, one might invent a new name, 'Ari$_{Fr}$' perhaps, and stipulate that it had exactly this sense. On the exam, students are asked, is it analytic that Ari$_{Fr}$ was a pupil of Plato's? The correct answer is "yes". Donnellan and Kripke show that ordinary proper names aren't required to have such senses, and ordinary ones in imperfect languages like English do not have them, not that there are no such senses available in the realm of Thought.

My arguments turned on the nonexistence of the senses needed, or more cautiously, the difficulty in finding them without resorting to senses of limited accessibility, which I thought was unnecessary to explain what was going on, implausible, and out of the spirit of Frege's insights about the realm of Thought. Kripke's arguments and mine lead to some of the same conclusions – for example, that Frege's theory doesn't quite work for imperfect languages. But the arguments differ. Indeed, a basic motivation for my puzzlement was that the characters seem to provide what names don't, modes of presentation tied to meaning and cognitive sigificance. But they don't quite provide what Frege needs, for these are only singular modes of presentation. So those of us convinced by Donnellan and Kripke about names had more work to do.

I thought that essential indexicals presented an additional problem for Frege, but also presented a problem for the new theories. The insights of Kripke and Donnellan lead to the problem of accounting for the differing cognitive significance of sentences with different proper names that express the same singular proposition. One response is that the difference is simply a matter of different names; everything else, like our reluctance to substitute in attitude reports, is a not a matter of semantics, but of pragmatics. But with indexicals, the problem was that we *do* seem to have an identifying conception of the referent, semantically identified by the character of the indexical, that does explain differences in cognitive significance. The hiker can regard "My favorite lake is Lake Gilmore" as true while not so regarding "That lake is Lake Gilmore" as false, because different modes of presentation are involved, revealed by the different characters. To be the referent of "my favorite lake," a lake has to be the lake the speaker prefers to all others at the time of utterance. To be the referent of "that lake," it has to be the lake the speaker is demonstrating or otherwise drawing attention to at the time of utterance.

Cappelen and Dever say:

> Perry points out that no Fregean substitution for "I" would give us a proposition with the same cognitive, motivational, and semantic effects as "I." No matter what the proposed substitution S is, it is only on the assumption that Perry also has the belief he would express by "I am S" that these effects are preserved. (p. 74)

The point is that "I" and other indexicals can be sensibly said to have "cognitive, motivational, and semantic effects" in virtue of their meanings. This is *not* what Donnellan and Kripke pointed out about proper names; it is almost the exact opposite. As I said above, proper names have a very thin cognitive significance. What explains our different reactions to different names is what we know about the referents beyond what is required to refer to them with the name, which is almost nothing. One doesn't even need to have understood the name used to use "whatchamacallit" to continue the chain and co-refer.

But in the case of indexicals, things are much different. If someone shouts "I need help," I will be motivated to move in the direction of the voice to see if I can help. The character of the indexical and the fact that I heard the shout provide me with the information necessary to act. If someone tells me, "Nadeem needs help," I will head from my office downstairs to his, even if the voice comes from another direction – even if it's on the phone. This has nothing to do with the meaning of "Nadeem"; it has to do with things I know about Nadeem – in this case, where his office is.

So suppose that Kripke and I agree that Fregean senses are not required, in either the case of proper names or indexicals, to secure reference. My arguments instantiate the same form as his: show cases of reference in which a Fregean sense is not involved. This does not show that my arguments are "simple instantiations of familiar and general objections to Fregeanism found in Kripke," and that criticism seems quite unwarranted. They show that, in addition to the agreed-upon fact that Fregean senses are not required for reference, indexicals provide an additional problem, not just for Frege, but for any version of the doctrine of propositions.

In fact, based on his articles "Frege's Theory of Sense and Reference" (2008) and "The First Person," (2011) I think that in fact Kripke and I do not agree, at least with respect to my criticisms of Frege. It seems that if my arguments were simple instantiations of his, he could hardly object to them. I suspect that ultimately our difference would come down to my commitment to a naturalistic account; as I pointed out above, if we give that up, some strategy based on senses of limited accessibility might work. But I do not claim to have yet fully understand this rich and subtle essay. Like our fellow Cornhusker Sandy Dennis, Kripke is incredible.

3 Some Thoughts About Pierre

Another famous essay by Kripke, "A Puzzle About Belief," raises an interesting challenge for my view. The heart of the essay is a puzzle about Pierre, with which readers are probably familiar. Growing up in Paris, Pierre read about London, in French, and came to assent to "Londres est jolie." Later he moves to London, learns English and based on his neighborhood, comes to assent to "London is not pretty." He doesn't realize that the city he is living in is the one he read about back in Paris. Pierre is a logician, very good at reasoning, but not all that interested in practical matters, like where he lives.

Kripke uses this example to generate a puzzle about belief for what I call "singular propositionalist" accounts that does not involve substitution or opacity. In addition to the facts of the example, we need two principles to generate the puzzle. The first is *Disquotation*:

> "If a normal English speaker, on reflection, sincerely assents to 'p,' then he believes that p." The sentence replacing 'p' is to lack indexical or pronomial devices or ambiguities that would ruin the intuitive sense of the principle. (Kripke 1979, pp. 248-9)

The second is *translation*:

> If a sentence of one language expresses a truth in that language, then any translation of it into any other language also expresses a truth (in that other language). (Kripke 1979, p. 250)

Given these principles, we seem to be able to conclude, with no appeal to substitution,

> Pierre believes that London is pretty
>
> Pierre believes that London is not pretty

The puzzle is, what should we say about this? Kripke goes over a number of candidate solutions with characteristic thoroughness and finds them wanting. At the end of his essay, the puzzle is still a puzzle.

Suppose that I were to propose something like this:

> Pierre believes both propositions. This makes it sound like he has contradictory beliefs. But he is in two different belief-states and believes that London is pretty in a different way than he believes that London is not pretty. It is the way a person believes propositions, not the propositions themselves, that is relevant to rationality.

Kripke says,

> It is no solution in itself to observe that some other terminology, which evades the question whether Pierre believes that London is pretty, may be sufficient to state all the relevant facts. (Kripke 1979, p. 259)

I don't evade the question whether Pierre believes that London is pretty. He does believe it, and he also believes that London isn't pretty.

Still, I think Kripke would think my proposal is (at best) a case of using other terminology to state the relevant facts, and so not a solution.

This seems correct, at least if I stick to the explanations for the terminology I offered in the first three essays in *The Problem of the Essential Indexical*. Using the terminology of "Belief and Acceptance," I would say that Pierre accepts "Londres est jolie" and "London is not pretty." We can classify a belief-state with the sentences it leads believers to regard as true – that is, the sentences it leads them to accept. Pierre isn't in a state that would lead him to accept "London is pretty and London is not pretty" nor in one that would lead him to accept "Londres est jolie et Londres n'est pas jolie." He is not irrational.

But this really just uses quotation with a couple of bells and whistles to describe the case. It doesn't explain how to describe the facts using "believes."

I think if we bring in some ideas from my essay with Mark Crimmins, "The Prince and the Phone Booth" (Chapter 12 of *The Problem of the Essential Indexical*), which I explained in the chapter on opacity, we do can better.

To review, first, we give up the doctrine of propositions. Beliefs aren't simply a relation between agents at times and propositions. They are episodes involving an agent being in a state at time or over a period of time involving various perturbations of the mind typically called "ideas." In particular, having a belief about an object, some idea or way of thinking about the object must be involved. It doesn't have to be a grasping of a Fregean sense. It could just be a name the believer uses to think about things, even things she knows nothing else about, like the student in my example. But it doesn't have to be a name. In my dialect of English, it could just be "whatchamacallit," or "whatsherface" or "whatshisname".

Second, our standard ways of reporting things systematically leave important parameters "unarticulated." This may be because they aren't or weren't known about. As I mentioned, "It's nine o'clock," with no reference *where* it is nine o'clock, worked fine for eons, before the relativity of time of day to location was relevant to conducting one's life. It still works fine for children and for the rest of us most of the time.

Third, language has ways of articulating such parameters, when they become important. Once we had trains that traveled fast enough to make the relativity of time of day to location relevant (such that travelers had to reset their watches) it was easy to start saying things like "It's noon here, so it must be about forty minutes earlier in Reno." Then time-zones were standardized, telegraphs, radio and television were invented, and "It's noon Pacific Standard Time" is now a standard form.

In the case of reporting beliefs and other attitudes, we have, or can introduce, ways of articulating usually unarticulated parameters. Crimmins and I use "via". Pierre believes, via his "Londres" idea, that London is pretty, but, via his "London" idea, believes that London is not pretty. I suggested in the opacity chapter that we could see Castañeda's quasi-indicators as a method of articulating such parameters. In ordinary English, there are less systematic ways. "Pierre believes that London is pretty, but only when he thinks of it as "Londres," not when he thinks of it as "London." In either case, we have additional terminology, but it is the the natural extension of the belief vocabulary, available when parameters usually left unarticulated are relevant, just as "in Reno" is a natural extension of the "o'clock" vocabulary when needed to clarify things.

So we can think of Kripke and other new theorists as a bit like railroads, modern phenomena who have forced us to cope with the fact that our system of attitude verbs and 'that'-clauses leaves important parameters of belief unarticulated. Just asking whether someone believes that London is pretty or doesn't is a bit like asking whether it is or isn't nine o'clock, without specifying a time zone. Most of the time, a yes or no answer will suffice, but not when we are traveling or dealing with Pierre.

I do not see my arguments as simple instantiations of Kripke's arguments, as indebted as I am to his writings. And I don't see why Cappelen and Dever do, either.

11

Back to Self-Knowledge

I'll now return to the issue of self-knowledge, looking at two places in Cappelen and Dever's book where this is discussed.

1   Nora and the Fax Machine

In Chapter 3, Cappelen and Dever quote from two of my later papers. The first, "Fodor and Psychological Explanations," I wrote with David Israel about a dozen years after "The Problem of the Essential Indexical." It was included in *The Problem of the Essential Indexical* (2000). The second, "Myself and I" (1998), was written about five years after that and was not included in the collection. They quote from the second paper, noting that they are adding a little boldface:

> In a later paper (1998), Perry says:
>
> > Consider a transaction with a fax machine. To press certain buttons on it, I have to move my fingers a certain distance and direction from me. It isn't enough to know where the buttons were relative to one another, or where the fax machine was in the building or room. I **had to know** where these things were relative to me (1998, p. 87)

On the basis of this quote, they credit me with some implausible views and two appropriately boldfaced fallacies and dismiss what I say as "rhetoric." Speaking of a fax machine user, they say:

> ... note that if she happens to think about the buttons' location relative to her, no argument has been given that she has to think about herself in a distinctly first-person way (whatever that means). If the agent is Nora and she happens to represent Nora's relationship to the buttons,

she could represent herself in a non-first-person way, e.g. as Nora.

In sum, there are at least two mistakes underlying Motivation 2. (Cappelen and Dever 2013, p. 44)

We'll look at Motivation 2 below.

2   Putting the Quote In Context

I think it is fair for me to explain the quote in light of the ideas and distinctions presented in the paper from which it was drawn. I'll begin with the entire passage from which their quote was drawn:

2.2 Knowledge Concerning the Self

Consider a simple successful transaction involving such a basic agent-relative role, and epistemic and pragmatic methods associated with it. I am hungry. I see an apple before me. I pick it up and eat it. The complex movement of arm, hand, fingers, neck and jaw was successful in getting the apple into my mouth, because of the distance and direction the apple was from me. What I learned from perception, then, must have been the distance and direction of the apple from me. Or consider a transaction with a fax machine. To press certain buttons on it, I have to move my fingers a certain distance and direction from me. It isn't enough to know where the buttons were relative to one another, or where the fax machine was in the building or the room. I had to know where these things were relative to me. (Perry 1998, p. 87)

To understand the passage, it is helpful to understand my terms "agent-relative role," "epistemic methods," and "pragmatic methods," which occur in the part Cappelen and Dever omitted. Also, understanding what I mean by "concerning" in the heading of the subsection is helpful. The sort of knowledge contemplated by my use of 'know' in the passage they boldface is clearly knowledge *concerning* the self. The section of which it is a subsection is titled "Agent-Relative Knowledge," and it would seem helpful to understand what I meant by that; I'll start there.

3   Agent-Relative Knowledge

The essay begins:

In this essay I distinguish three kinds of self-knowledge. I call these three kinds agent-relative knowledge, self-attached knowledge and knowledge of the person one happens to be. These aspects of self-knowledge differ in how the knower or agent is represented. Most of what I say will be applicable to beliefs as well as knowledge, and to other kinds of attitudes and thoughts, such as desire, as well.

Agent-relative knowledge is knowledge from the perspective of a particular agent. To have this sort of knowledge, the agent need not have an idea of self, or a notion of himself or herself. This sort of knowledge can be expressed by a simple sentence containing a demonstrative for a place or object, and without any term referring to the speaker. For example, "There is an apple" or "that is a toaster". (Perry 1998, p. 83)

I regard agent-relative knowledge – what I now usually call "primitive self-knowledge" – as widespread in nature. It doesn't require language, or an articulated mental life involving ideas of the things known about or the knower. When a chicken sees a kernel of corn in front of her, she has agent-relative knowledge of the location of the kernel relative to her. As I see it, the chicken's perceptual states have veridicality conditions. If the perception is veridical, there is a kernel of corn a certain distance and direction in front of her at the time of the perception; if there isn't, it's not. Chickens that are in that perceptual state, in normal conditions, will walk that distance and direction and peck. That's how their internal architecture works. Other chickens in the same perceptual state will do the same. This isn't armchair reasoning. Over the years, I've spread kernels of corn in front of hundreds of chickens and watched them strut and peck.

This is an example of what Israel and I call "harnessing information" in "What is Information," (1990) the first paper in a series of which the Fodor paper was the second. The basic idea comes from Dretske and was developed in my book with Jon Barwise, *Situations and Attitudes*, and then further developed by Israel and me. A system *harnesses* information about its environment when three conditions are met: (a) it has sensors or something like sensors that can be in range of states, depending on the external environment; (b) the states of these sensors carry information about states of the environment, in the sense that given the operative constraints and normal circumstances, the sensors will be in a certain state only if the environment is in a certain state, or at least the sensor's state confers a significant probability that the environment is in the corresponding state; (c) the architecture of the system is such that being in a given state causes changes in the system that promote some value, given relevant constraints, and given the information being harnessed. In the chicken's case, the states of its eyes carry information about the presence or absence of kernels of corn in various directions at various distances, given that it is in a normal barnyard. Given the way chickens work, this causes it to walk the appropriate distance in the appropriate direction and peck, which promotes the value of getting nutrition.

If I say, of a certain chicken, "She sees that there is a kernel of corn in front of her," I use a proposition to classify her perceptual state in terms of its veridicality conditions. The chicken herself is what I call an "unarticulated constituent" of the proposition I use for this purpose. That means there is nothing in the chicken's mental state, no perturbation of consciousness, no "mental indexical," no idea, that refers to her and accounts for her being a constituent of the proposition.

The state of the chicken's eyes carry all sorts of information about the world, given various constraints. Given the right constraints, it probably indicates something about how chickens evolved. But not all of the information carried is harnessed. What we are looking for is the *additional* or *incremental* information about those factors in her environment that are relevant to the success of her pecking. *Her* pecking will be successful in providing *her* nutrition if there is a kernel of corn in front of *her*. That's why *she* is in the proposition that provides the veridicality conditions of her perception. In my terminology, she is an unarticulated constituent of the veridicality conditions of her perception, and for this reason she doesn't have knowledge *about* herself, but only *concerning* herself; thus the heading of the section from which the quote was taken.

Consider an incident that involved George W. Bush. While he was giving a speech in Iraq, an Iraqi journalist threw a shoe at him. He ducked. As I analyze it, he had agent-relative knowledge that there was a shoe coming at his head, and this caused him to duck, which promoted the value of his not getting hit in the face with a shoe. This was, as we say, reactive and automatic. But it was also motivated and rational. He had a reason to duck. He didn't want to get hit in the face with a shoe. He saw that there was a shoe coming at him then. Given that he is a normal human being, the desire and the perception caused him to duck.

He didn't have to say to himself, "There is a shoe coming at me now," much less "There is a shoe coming at President Bush now." He didn't have to think such a thought in mentalese or with "mental indexicals." If he had, he might not have ducked in time. Luckily, it was a case of "agent-relative knowledge" – that is, "primitive self-knowledge." Even Presidents need primitive self-knowledge.

Now suppose that a moment or two later he is asked what happened. He says, "Someone threw a shoe at me." This would exhibit what I called "self-attached knowledge." It requires he have some idea or conception or, as I would say, *notion* of himself. Our self-notion is the normal repository for information acquired in what I call "normally self-informative ways" – that is, "epistemic methods" like perception, interoception, and the others I mentioned in discussing Frege – that contain information about the agent employing them. And such notions motivate what I call "normally self-effecting ways of acting" – that is, pragmatic methods that have an effect on the agent who employs them and objects with various relations to the agent. These can be based on the combination of beliefs picked up in normally self-informative ways at the time of acting together with all sorts of additional information stored in the self-notion. Humans typically have rich self-notions. I may underestimate them, but I don't think chickens do. But whether you throw a shoe at a chicken or a President, it will dodge the shoe, and in neither case does a self-notion need to be involved in our explanation of the appropriate avoidance behavior.

Now suppose much later, after he has almost forgotten about the shoe thrown at him in Iraq, Bush sees a rather indistinct video of the incident. He does recognize himself in the video. He says, "That man had shoe coming at his face. You know, I seem to remember something like that happening to me once."

In this case, Bush has what I call "knowledge of the person one happens to be." He knows, of the man he sees in the video, that the man had a shoe coming at his face at the time the video was taken. And the man in the video is him. He is constituent of the singular proposition he expressed with "That man had a shoe coming at his face." But he doesn't know this in the *way* we normally know things about ourselves. It's not integrated into his self-notion.

The paper with Israel was written about a dozen years after "The Problem of the Essential Indexical." In between, Jon Barwise and I had developed situation semantics, which incorporated all of the views espoused in that paper in a "relational theory of meaning." The relational theory of meaning was basically a variation on Kaplan's theory. Meanings were relations between discourse situations and what we called interpretations, rather than functions from contexts to contents as in Kaplan's theory, and interpretations were sets of situations rather than sets of possible worlds. A bit later, I developed the idea of "unarticulated constituents," and Mark Crimmins and I used in the paper mentioned in Chapter 9 to improve the theory of propositional attitude reports given in *Situations and Attitudes*. And Israel and I had developed a theory of incremental information based on our version of situation semantics. These developments, all explained in *The Problem of the Essential Indexical*, involved new ideas and terminology, but the doctrines of "The Problem of the Essential Indexical" remained unmolested, as they do in my account of self-knowledge. The distinction between *how* and *what* remains central. Propositions get at *what* is believed, known, perceived, accomplished, etc. by articulating their truth, veridicality, or success conditions. Roles get at the *how*. The connection between roles and contents is due to the fact that the agent who is in the state and executes the movements provides the arguments for the roles that determined the contents.

4 Back to Nora

Motivation 2 is **Bodily Movements Require Indexical Thoughts**. Recall that in the quote above Cappelen and Dever say of Nora and me:

> no argument has been given that she has to think about herself in a distinctly first-person way (whatever that means).

After discussing Nora, they continue by attributing a couple of bold-face fallacies to me:

> In sum, there are at least two mistakes underlying Motivation 2.
>
> **Over-Representation Fallacy.** Because the body is involved in the movement, the body needs to be mentally represented.
>
> **Relational Fallacy.** If some part of the body has to be represented, it has to be indexically represented.
>
> There simply are no arguments or evidence for either of these claims. Not everything involved in an action needs to be represented by the actor. And even if you maintain that some part of the body has to be represented, it doesn't follow that it has to be indexically represented. What's important is just that it gets represented, so that it can be directed or controlled. Indexicality just seems to be irrelevant. (Cappelen and Dever 2013, p. 44)

It's up to Cappelen and Dever to tell us what they mean by "distinctly first-person way." I don't use the phrase. I do note in the essay that Sydney Shoemaker uses "first-person knowledge" for what I call "self-attached knowledge" — that is, for exactly what I claim *need not be* involved pushing the fax button, which only requires agent-relative knowledge, knowledge *concerning* the self.

With regard to the boldfaced fallacies, I don't see that they have anything to do with the views I express in the essay — other than being claims I show to be false. I don't know what they mean by "represented" or "indexically represented." If it simply means that different agents at different times represent different information by being in the same state, then they owe us an explanation of why they deny this plausible claim. If they mean that some kind of mental indexical or internal recitation of a sentence containing indexicals needs to be involved, I don't say that, or anything close to it. The term "concerning" in the title of the paragraph from which their quote is drawn makes it clear that I don't commit the two fallacies.

So, I am tempted to conclude that not only did Cappelen and Dever not read all of "The Problem of the Essential Indexical," or at least they quit paying attention once they began to free associate, they extended the same standard of scholarship to "Myself and I."

5   Immunity to Error Through Misidentfication

Cappelen and Dever return to the topic of self-knowledge in Chapter 7, "Indexicality and Immunity to Error."

Immunity to error through misidentification is Sydney Shoemaker's name for a phenomenon that would seem undeniable, had Cappelen and Dever not denied it. As John Locke said some time ago:

> When we see, hear, smell, taste, feel, meditate, or will anything, we know that we do so. It is always like that with our present sensations and perceptions. And it is through this that everyone is to himself that which he calls 'self' ...

Not only Shoemaker, but Descartes, Locke, Kant, and many other philosophers accepted some form of the doctrine of immunity. (Just for the record, none of them were influenced by my unclear theses couched in ill-defined terminology.)

When a person learns that someone is in pain by having a pain, she knows that she herself is in pain. When a person learns that someone has their legs crossed through being in the proprioceptive state one in when one's legs are crossed, the person they learn about is themselves. I say that being in such states are "normally self-informative" ways of finding out that someone is in pain or has their legs crossed. If one in such states says, "I am in pain" or "My legs are crossed," they will be right. "Immunity" I take to mean that in anything approaching normal conditions, the person will know it is she herself who is in pain or has her legs crossed.

Things can be pretty abnormal without undermining this immunity. Consider Castañeda's war hero, call him Elwood. Elwood performed heroic deeds in a battle, was injured, lost his dog-tags, acquired amnesia, and wandered far from the battle. He ends up in a military hospital, for it is clear that he is a G.I., although there is no telling what his name is or his unit was. In Castañeda's story, Elwood goes on to write a biography about the hero in a battle that occurred the same day he lost his memory, without ever realizing that it was really an autobiography. But I am interested in the first part of the story, when Elwood is in the hospital.

In a perfectly straightforward sense, Elwood doesn't know who he is. He doesn't know his name, or anything very distinctive about himself, except that he has amnesia and is in a hospital, which could also be true of other patients. Now suppose the nurse brings him dinner. He feels hunger. Does he know which mouth he needs to put the food in, to relieve the hunger? Does he know how to move the limbs in the way required to get the food in the correct mouth? It seems he does. Elwood has agent-relative knowledge or primitive self-knowledge, even though he doesn't have self-attached knowledge, or at least not much of it in his early days in the hospital, when he is building up a new self-notion almost from scratch. If Elwood learns, through visceroception, that someone needs to urinate, he will know who needs to proceed to the restroom. When he so proceeds, he will explain what he is doing to the nurse by saying "I need to visit the restroom." So, even in these decidedly abnormal circumstances, we have immunity to error through misidentification when he learns about someone through interoception, proprioception, visceroception, and other normally self-informative methods. And in this sense, he will know who is seeing the things he learns about visually, or who is hearing the things he hears.

But we can imagine even more abnormal cases, where interventions have been made in the central nervous system of two individuals, so one feels the need to urinate when the other's bladder is full. This wouldn't pass the Human Subjects Committee, but I wouldn't be surprised if it had been done to cats or even monkeys.

So I don't want to claim that the immunity in question is a matter of necessity. My respect for the ability of philosophers to come up with possible counterexamples makes me very leery of claims of necessity. Daniel Dennett, another eminent philosopher whom Cappelen and Dever see as taken in by my rhetoric, gives us a symphony of such cases in his brilliant article, "Where Am I?" (1981). But I think that in the course of human history so far, there have been very few cases, if any, where a person learns facts about someone else via introspection, proprioception, interoception, visceroception, and other normally self-informative ways of finding out what's happening. That's what I mean by "Immunity to error through misidentification." I think it is true, and philosophically interesting, as is the fact that the first person is the natural way for people to express what they learn by these methods.

6   Inflate and Puncture

Cappelen and Dever's book often exhibits the strategy I call "inflate and puncture." One takes an interesting claim some philosopher makes, inflates it beyond recognition, and then punctures the inflated claim. They apply this method to Shoemaker's conception of immunity to error, regarding it as a claim about necessary truth.

Thesis 1 is "There is no Immunity to Error Through Misidentification."

> Here is our central argument for Thesis 1: no claim, including (*) ["I am in pain"], is epistemically privileged in this way. Suppose Gareth believes that his legs are crossed on the basis of proprioceptive awareness. He could, of course, be wrong about the state of his legs (his proprioception could be malfunctioning), but the received wisdom is that he could not be wrong about whose legs are (purportedly) crossed. But suppose Gareth has, through some science-fiction mechanism, been wired up so that he sometimes receives proprioceptive input from John's legs. Then, when Gareth has proprioceptive awareness as of his legs being crossed, he should be, if he is aware of his deviant wiring, uncertain whether it is his legs or John's legs that are being proprioceptively represented as being crossed. So even if Gareth has not been deviantly wired, he is not immune to error, because until the

possibility of deviant wiring has been eliminated, the possibility of error due to misidentification cannot be eliminated. There is clearly a general recipe here: for any of Gareth's beliefs about himself and any source of evidence for that belief, we can imagine him being such that he sometimes receives evidence of that sort from someone else's state. (Cappelen and Dever 2013, p. 131)

This is irrelevant to what I mean by "immunity to error through misidentification" or, as far as I can tell, what anyone except Cappelen and Dever mean by it. Adopting their technique, I suggest they are committed to a couple of false boldface claims:

CP-1 Interesting philosophical claims are limited to claims that some truth is necessary. It is not enough that the truth it is contingently pervasive, has had an important role in formulating our ordinary concepts and practices, or even played a key role in evolution.

CP-2 The only kind of epistemic privilege of any interest is the sort involved in knowing necessary truths.

I think these are both quite absurd.

7 Recanati's Account

Cappelen and Dever consider an account of immunity to error given by François Recanati, another philosopher taken in by my rhetoric and the arguments I paraded. Recanati says:

... Immunity to error through misidentification characterizes thoughts that are "implicitly" *de se*, as opposed to thoughts that involve an explicit self-identification. Thoughts that are implicitly *de se* involve no reference to the self at the level of content: what makes them *de se* is simply the fact that the content of the thought is evaluated with respect to the thinking subject ... We end up with a threefold taxonomy. First, there are accidental *de se* thoughts, namely thoughts that are about an individual x who happens to be oneself. Second, there are genuine *de se* thoughts – the sort of thought one expresses by using the first-person and which, for that reason, I call "first-person thoughts." In this category we must distinguish between explicit and implicit *de se* thoughts. Explicit *de se* thoughts are a variety of *de re* thoughts and give rise to Frege cases, while implicit *de se* thoughts are not and do not. (2007, pp. 4-5)

Recanati sometimes uses terminology I tend to avoid, but he always explains it clearly. He uses Lewis's term '*de se*' but then distinguishes an important difference that I think '*de se*' and 'self-ascription' obscure, between agent-relative or primitive self-knowlege and self-attached knowledge. In my terms, what Recanati calls "accidental *de se* thoughts" are cases of knowledge of the person one happens to be. What he calls "genuine *de se* thought" are what I call self-attached knowledge. What he calls "implicit *de se* thoughts" are primitive self-knowledge.

So the point he makes seem exactly right. Immunity to error characterizes thoughts that are implicitly *de se* – that is, thoughts that are self-locating without involving self-attached knowledge

Cappelen and Dever's discussion of Recanati uses another technique I call "quote and ignore." Regarding immunity they say,

> There is no obvious need for a concept of the self, or for any indexicality, to be involved.

But who said there was? Recanati explicitly denies this, in the very passage they quote. It is implicit *de se* thoughts, what I call primitive self knowledge, that is involved. And who said indexicality was involved in having knowledge by proprioception or interoception? The connection is simply that because the way of knowing is normally knowledge about the knower's limbs or bladder or stomach, and because of the characters of indexicals, such knowledge is naturally expressed, by animals that have mastered English and have some notion of themselves, by statements using 'I'. But anyone who has taken a dog for a walk knows that dogs have normally self-informative experiences that lead to normally self-effecting actions, like urinating on the neighbor's flowers, without ever saying much of anything. Are they immune to error? I've never seen a dog make a mistake about which dog needed to urinate when it felt the need to do so.

8 More Inflating and Puncturing

A heading of one section of their discussion is "Thesis 3: Indexicality Does Not Explain Immunity." As I use the term 'indexical', indexicals are expressions in natural language, and indexicality is the sort of context-sensitivity that they exhibit and Kaplan's theory explains.

Why would anyone think that indexicality, a feature of language, explains immunity to error through misidentification, a phenomenon that pervades all life and is essential to evolution? Immunity to error through misidentification extends to animals that evolved eons before language appeared on the horizon. There are certain things that the most primitive of animals simply don't need to worry about. Chickens don't need to worry about whether the kernels they see are in front of them or some other chicken, or whether the pangs of hunger they feel will be relieved by their eating the kernels they see. That's one reason they don't need the intellectual equipment required to have such worries. Indexicality has absolutely nothing to do with the fact that the information chickens pick up from perception and visceroception is in anything like normal conditions information about the very chicken picking up the information.

The connection with indexicality is simply that which I argued for in my essays. We need to distinguish between ways of knowing and what is known. As theorists, we need to credit each chicken with knowledge *concerning* itself – primitive self-knowledge, with the chicken as an unarticulated constituent – that secures the conditions of success of the pecking it causes. And we need to recognize that different chickens know different things, *concerning* different chickens, in the same way. When we are dealing with literate human beings, their use of indexicals may convey *how* they believe or know things, in addition to identifying *what* they believe or know. Immunity is part of the explanation of the importance of indexicals, not the other way around.

Some philosophers, including Recanati at times, use "indexicality" not only for the linguistic phenomenon, but for the pattern it exemplifies, the distinction between how and what. I think this is susceptible to misinterpretation. But if we use "indexicality" in this way, carefully severing any dependance of the phenomenon of indexicality so understood on language, the ability to use context-sensitive expressions, or having some sort of self-notion, perhaps indexicality does explain immunity. I would prefer to say that immunity, the possession of animals of normally self-informative methods of knowing, explains the importance of indexicality, a device that language users employ to disclose beliefs acquired through such normally self-informative methods.

12

Lewis's Theory

1 Points of Agreement

In his article "Attitudes *De Dicto* and *De Se*" (1979), David Lewis puts forward an account of belief that he takes to have much in common with the view I put forward in "Frege on Demonstratives."

We agree in modifying the first tenet of the doctrine of propositions, that belief *consists* in being in relation to a proposition. My modification allowed propositions a reasonably important place. They get at *what* is believed, but they don't get at the *ways* of believing. Believing induces a relation to propositions, which encode at the truth-conditions of beliefs, taking into account both the internal structure of the beliefs and their external circumstances. I did not hold that believing *consists in* having a relation to some *other* abstract object rather than a proposition. My roles are not the *objects* of beliefs, but ways of classifying belief states that don't depend on external facts and illuminate their connections with perception and action.

In the usual interpretation, which fits with his terminology – but, I will argue, not with everything he says – Lewis holds that belief *does* consist in a relation between believers and abstract objects. But these abstract objects are not propositions but rather properties that a person might have at a time. Believing consists in the *self-ascription* of properties. Self-ascription is an attitude towards such properties. Such properties, unlike at least many propositions, are "in the head."

There is nothing like the concept of self-ascription, so interpreted, in my account.

However, the properties Lewis sees us as self-ascribing and the roles I see as classifying belief states seem to be basically the same abstract objects. In my view, when I straightened up the sack in my cart in the supermarket, I was in a belief state that can be classified by the role that takes us from the believer and the time of the belief to the singular proposition that *the believer has a torn sack of sugar at the time of the belief*. My belief was true because I had a torn sack of sugar in my cart at the time of belief. In Lewis's theory, I self-ascribed the property *x has a torn sack of sugar at t*. This self-ascription was true because I had a torn sack of sugar in my cart at the time I made it.

So there is an important point of agreement, but also an important point of disagreement, on the usual interpretation of Lewis's view.

Lewis's view is not entirely clear, because he uses the term "object of belief" in a very special way. Usually one takes objects of belief and other attitudes to be the references of 'that'-clauses in attitude reports. But on Lewis's usage, the term is used for those objects that capture the causal roles of beliefs. I do not use the term in this way and consider Lewis's usage to be confusing.

In my view, there are two ways of classifying beliefs and three sorts of abstract objects needed to do so. First, there are qualitative propositions, such as Frege's Thoughts or Lewis's sets of possible worlds with no shared individuals. Second, there are circumstances or singular propositions. In an account like Kaplan's, where possible worlds have overlapping domains of individuals, sets of possible worlds can provide both qualitative and singular propositions.

In ordinary attitude reports, beliefs are classified by propositions, the references of 'that'-clauses, which I call "what is believed" and would call the "objects of belief" if I used that term. Propositions do not capture the causal role of different types of belief states and, do not capture (all of) the cognitive significance of the sentences an agent will use to express her beliefs. We need to supplement our account of belief with *roles*, which are functions from agents and times to propositions, which I call *ways* of believing. The role of a belief, together with the agent, time, and circumstances of the belief, determine what is believed.

In Lewis's view, there is one way of classifying beliefs, by the properties the believer must have at the time of belief for the belief to be true. As I pointed out, these classifying properties are more or less equivalent to roles, generalizing Kaplan's characters. They classify beliefs in ways that fit with their causal roles, and they provide truth-conditions. If the truth-conditions determine qualitative propositions, the beliefs are *de dicto*. If they only provide conditions on the agent or the time, they are *irreducibly de se*.

If I say, "I am making a mess now," I express what Lewis calls an irreducibly *de se* belief, because the truth-conditions provided are conditions on the agent and time. If I say, "I am making a mess at noon central time on December 12, 1963," I still express such an irreducibly *de se* belief. But if I say, "The only philosophy major in the Crete, Nebraska Safeway store at noon central time on December 12, 1963 is making a mess at that time," I may manage to express a *de dicto* belief. Lewis does not recognize singular propositions; he recognizes a phenomenon called "*de re* belief" but regards it not as belief, but as a complex property involving beliefs plus relations of acquaintance or, in some cases, essences.

The main point on which Lewis agrees with me is that we need to classify beliefs in terms of roles or classifying properties; qualitative propositions alone don't do the job. It is this point of agreement that Cappelen and Dever object to. I'll consider their objections, then turn to some differences between Lewis and me, and then further discuss the correct interpretation of Lewis.

Lewis uses my Hume/Heimson and Lingens cases to argue for this point, and in addition supplies an example in which two gods on different mountains both know all true qualitative propositions, but neither knows which god he is.

2 Cappelen and Dever on Lewis

Over many years of conversation with David Lewis and study of his writing, I developed a concept I call "Lewis-speak." He constructed a brilliant framework for thinking about philosphical issues, but it is often difficult, at least for me, to appreciate his insights without some effort to get inside his framework. For example, he says, "Beliefs *de re* are not really beliefs." He is making a valid point, within his framework and his terminology, by saying something that on the face of it seems clearly false. For me at any rate, finding the insights behind what Lewis says and translating them into a framework I find plausible is often a (worthwhile) struggle.

It seems to me that Cappelen and Dever also struggle. Their task is not made easier by describing Lewis's view with terms he doesn't use and not paying attention to the limits of his topic that he explains in this footnote:

> [16] That is why it seems to me unfortunate that the study of the objects of belief has become entangled with the semantic analysis of attributions of belief. I hope that in this paper I have managed to keep the topics separate. (Lewis 1979, p. 541)

For example, Cappelen and Dever write:

> Of course, Lewis does have a general account of opacity, but it is a general account that gives indexicality and the *de se* a special and central place. So the question is: why think that problems of opacity call for this kind of indexicalized content? Lewis does not give us any reason to think that his indexical versions of Frege puzzles are special in any way, so we're left with no reason for thinking that the solution to Frege puzzles is to say that we think of all objects indirectly, by thinking about ourselves. (p. 100)

Opacity simply isn't what Lewis is talking about, as is clear from the way he limits his topic in the footnote. The words "opacity" and "opaque" do not occur in the article. In keeping with his footnote, "Attitudes *De Dicto* and *De Se*" doesn't tell us about what his general account of opacity is or whether it treats the substitution of indexicals differently than it treats the substitution of proper names. Insofar as

Lewis presents us with "indexical versions of Frege puzzles," they are puzzles about cognitive significance, not opacity.

At one point, they ask:

> Lewis's view that attitude contents are properties is certainly a revisionary theory of content, but why is it an indexical theory of content? (p. 91)

In his essay, Lewis uses the words "contented" and "discontented" a number of times to describe the moods that various proposals put him in or perhaps should put him in. He uses "content" once, in a footnote about Kaplan. He never describes his own view in terms of "content," much less "indexical content." The term "indexical" occurs twice, in a description of a view he doesn't hold, but does not occur at all in his explanations of his own view. This seems rather remarkable, if Lewis's essay is a prime example of advocacy of "essential indexicality."

My focus is whether Cappelen and Dever undermine the case Lewis makes for the view he and I share but I express in quite different ways; as I put it, roles characterize belief states in a way that reflects their causal roles and cognitive significance.

As I said, Lewis uses three cases, his "two-gods" case and two cases from "Frege on Demonstratives": the Lingens case and the Hume/Heimson case.

Cappelen and Dever's discussion of the two-gods case goes in a number of different directions involving the *possible worlds* framework that I won't try to unravel. There was one comment, however, that I found especially odd.

> Recall that for Lewis's two gods argument to work, it is crucial that the propositionally omniscient gods still do not know who and where they are. Suppose Zeus is the god on the tallest mountain and Odin is the god on the coldest mountain. Then Zeus, despite his propositional omniscience, does not know that he is the god on the tallest mountain. He does, however, presumably know that Zeus is the god on the tallest mountain. There is a straightforward possible-worlds content to be assigned to the belief that Zeus is the god on the tallest mountain. (p. 99)

It's not clear to me what this straightforward possible worlds content would be. It can't be the set of possible worlds in which Zeus is the god on the tallest mountain, or the god in fact called "Zeus" is the god on the tallest mountain. In Lewis's theory of possible worlds, all concrete individuals, even gods, are world-bound. The only world in the set would be the actual world, since the actual world is the only one in which Zeus is to be found. One would have to settle for the set of worlds in which the Zeus counterparts are the god on the tallest mountain. But there is nothing absolute about the counterpart relation; it is dependent on the context of inquiry. Whatever content they have in mind, it doesn't seem to be straightforward.

The two gods lead Cappelen and Dever back to the liefmotif of their book, a confusion between opacity and cognitive significance, encapsulated in the term "Frege Puzzle":

> So what Lewis is trying to explain is how Zeus can know that Zeus is the god on the tallest mountain, but not know that he is the god on the tallest mountain. But this, of course, is just a special case of traditional Frege puzzles. (p. 99)

Lewis's most extended defense of our common view occurs in his discussion of the Hume-Heimson case, which is not a traditional Frege puzzle. It doesn't involved substitution of one referring expression for another changing cognitive significance, and it certainly has nothing to do with opacity. Cappelen and Dever apparently originally intended to ignore it but were pressed to address it by Juhani Yli-Vakkuri, and thus dealt with it in a footnote.

Lewis first notes that there is no possible world where Hume and Heimson are literally identical, they could be at most vicariously identical in virtue of having a common counterpart, since they have little in common. He then meanders around a bit before getting to the main point:

> Doubtless it is true in some sense that Heimson does not believe what Hume did. But there had better also be a central and important sense in which Heimson and Hume believe alike. For one thing, the predicate "believes he is Hume" applies alike to both: Heimson believes he is Hume, and Hume believes he is Hume. Do not say that I equivocate, and that what is true is only that Heimson believes that he (Heimson) is Hume and Hume believes that he (Hume) is Hume. Everyone believes that Hume is Hume, but not everyone

believes that he – he himself – is Hume. There is a genuine, univocal predicate, which appears for instance in "Not everyone believes that he is Hume," and that is the predicate that applies alike to Heimson and Hume. (Lewis 1979, p. 525)

After saying this, Lewis goes off topic for a bit. He brings up the need for the semantics of attitude reports to provide an account of "Not everyone believes that he is Hume." He then, as was his wont, pontificates a bit about beliefs being in the head, before returning to his argument and stating his conclusion:

> The solution is that the object is not a proposition at all. It is a property: the property of being Hume. Hume self-ascribes this property; he has it; he is right. Heimson, believing just what Hume does, self-ascribes the very same property; he lacks it; he is wrong. (Lewis 1979, p. 526)

If we keep in mind Lewis's special use of 'object', the conclusion is that the property of being David Hume is what we need to get at the aspect that Hume's belief and Heimson's belief have in common, given that their beliefs have different truth-conditions and truth-values.

In their earlier discussion of the Hume/Heimson case, Cappelen and Dever admitted they couldn't find a "Fregean Counterpart" and concluded the case must be irrelevant. Thus, in their footnote on Lewis's use of it, they do not give a Fregean Counterpart. Instead, they discuss an irrelevancy Lewis introduced in his meanderings. Lewis says, in the off-topic part of his discussion,

> … Heimson may have got his head into perfect match with Hume's in every way that is at all relevant to what he believes. If nevertheless Heimson and Hume do not believe alike, then *beliefs ain't in the head!* (Lewis 1979, p. 525)

Having constructed a Putnam "twin case," Lewis then launches into criticisms of what new theorist of reference say and what Hilary Putnam said about such cases. This is all irrelevant to his conclusion.

Cappelen and Dever say:

> Since we don't, and don't see any reason to, endorse the claim that all content is narrow content, we reject a crucial premise of the argument, and don't see it as a compelling motivation for a thesis of Essential Indexicality. We would also note that it's far from obvious that Heimson can get his head into a perfect match with Hume's while

at the same time believing, unlike Hume, that Heimson is Hume. (p. 88)

They may be right about the second point, but that's irrelevant. The Hume/Heimson case was not a Putnam twin-case, and Lewis's turning it into such a case served no purpose in the argument for what they call "Essential Indexicality," nor does Lewis claim that it does. It is very far from being a premise, much less a crucial one. The purpose it serves is allowing him to vent a bit about Putnam, new theorists of reference, and beliefs being in the head.

What about the first point, about "narrow content"? This is a phrase Lewis doesn't use, drawn from the confusing and confused literature on "externalism" and "internalism."

I think these issues are greatly clarified by the distinction made in "The Problem of the Essential Indexical" between the what and the how of assertion and belief. In my account, using "content" as Kaplan does, the content of Heimson's assertion "I am David Hume" is a singular proposition with Heimson and Hume as constituents. The property of being Hume is in the singular proposition because of a relation that Heimson's assertion and belief have to a long-dead philosopher, which clearly involves facts outside of Heimson's head and so is not fully determined by events inside of his head. On my view, the content of Heimson's belief is clearly not in the head, in any reasonable sense. But that is not to say that beliefs are not in the head.

What one who is impressed by the arguments I give for "Essential Indexicality" needs to accept is only that what one might call the "narrow" causal roles of belief states will be determined by what goes on in the head and the central nervous system. The fact that the belief-state of Hume and Heimson causes both of them, as competent speakers of English, to say "I am David Hume," is due to what goes on inside brains and central nervous systems. If Hume never existed, and there were no singular proposition to serve as the content of Heimson's belief, he would utter the same sentence. And this is all one needs to accept Lewis's arguments.

Lewis's use of the Hume/Heimson case to argue for the thesis he expresses, in Lewis-Speak, by saying that the objects of the attitudes are properties, depends on the premise that beliefs are in the head, and their local causal roles are determined by the states of the head. Whatever Lewis would say using the term "narrow content," and whatever Cappelen and Dever mean the phrase to mean, is quite irrelevant.

Lewis also discusses my case of Rudolf Lingens:

> An amnesiac, Rudolf Lingens, is lost in the Stanford library. He reads a number of things in the library, including a biography of himself, and a detailed account of the library in which he is lost ... He still won't know who he is, and where he is, no matter how much knowledge he piles up, until that moment when he is ready to say, "This place is aisle five, floor six, of Main Library, Stanford. I am Rudolf Lingens." (Perry 1977, p. 492)

Cappelen and Dever refer us to their earlier discussion of the Lingens case to deal with Lewis's use of it. In this earlier discussion, they say that with a bit of thought one can see "... we are faced with nothing but a familiar Frege puzzle case." They then clinch their case with a "Fregean Counterpart":

> We are trying to locate Superman. We are in the Stanford library, and read a number of things in the library, including a biography of Clark Kent. We believe any Fregean thought you think might help us. We still won't know that Clark Kent is Superman no matter how much knowledge we pile up, until that moment when we are ready to say, "Superman is Clark Kent." (p. 63)

As noted, the relevance of "Fregean Counterparts" is based on Cappelen and Dever's confusion of opacity and cognitive significance. Lingens reads "Rudolf Lingens is lost in the Stanford Library" and hence might say "I believe that Lingens is lost in the Stanford Library." If we replace 'Lingens' with 'I,' we obtain "I believe that I am lost in the Stanford Library." He wouldn't say that. If we believe in opacity, we'll say that the reports have different truth-values. If we don't, we'll say that the second report is extremely misleading.

Somewhat similarly, if I don't know that Clark Kent is Superman, I may say, "I believe that Superman was born on Krypton," but not be willing to say, "I believe Clark Kent was born in Krypton." We have either opacity or the appearance of opacity in both cases. The appropriate response to this argument seems to be: "So what?"

Neither Lewis nor I were talking about opacity. Using my terminology, we were talking about cognitive significance. Lingens regarded "Lingens is lost in the Stanford Library" as true and did not so regard "I am lost in the Stanford Library." In the Counterpart, I regarded "Superman was born on Krypton" as true but did not so regard "Clark Kent was born on Krypton." In both cases, we have differences in cognitive significance. If one accepts Kripke's account of names and Kaplan's account of indexicals, the account for the differences in the two cases will be quite different. If one accepts Frege's account of proper names in "On Sense and Reference" and his account of indexicals in "The Thought," the accounts will be quite different. Cappelen and Dever apparently have a non-Fregean account, but until they tell us more about it, it is hard to accept their apparent view that changes in cognitive significance due to substitution of co-referential expressions for indexicals do not raise interesting issues not raised by substitution of names for names. And it is even harder to accept their view that cases, like the Hume/Heimson case, in which two believers regard he same sentence as true, one by virtue of a false belief and he other by virtue of a true belief, raise no interesting issues. Until they tell us more about their own theory, they have given us no reason to reject Lewis's arguments.

3 A Point of Disagreement

Lewis claims that my view is needlessly complex, because I recognize two ways of classifying beliefs (two "objects of belief" in his sense): the role associated with the belief, and the proposition an agent at a time believes in virtue of being in such a state in certain circumstances. I think his objection is connected with his disapproval of seeing "*de re* beliefs" as beliefs. Lewis and I agree that beliefs are in the head, or at least the head and the rest of the central nervous system. I don't think it follows from this that the abstract objects we use to classify beliefs need to be in the head. I don't see why roles or classifying properties are in the head in any very clear sense; the important thing is that they provide a way of classifying beliefs that does not depend on external circumstances, which is important for certain purposes, such as understanding their causal roles. But ways of classifying beliefs that depend on external circumstances can be quite useful.

Folk psychology was a concept that Lewis, David Armstrong, and others put forward in various forms. We can think of the concepts and vocabulary we have for describing the mind as something like a theory, developed over eons by the folk, long before they knew that the brain had much to do with it. It works remarkably well for describing what is going on in our minds and others, given how little the folk knew about how things worked.

But I think of this theory as "folk psychology and communication theory" rather than merely "folk psychology." Folk theory gives us concepts and vocabulary that are not only useful in describing what goes on in one's mind, but also how information is passed from person to person. I think that emphasizing the latter use provides a better understanding of how the vocabulary and concepts of the theory work. In particular, it makes sense of the fact that circumstances or singular propositions often turn out to be the "objects of belief," in what I regard as the correct use of that phrase, if one is going to use it at all – that is, as the references of 'that'-clauses.

As discussed above, in his *Begriffsschrift*, Frege took sentences to refer to circumstances, a species of singular propositions. Or, more carefully, he adopted the common-sense position, which, from the perspective of more than a hundred years later, can be described as thinking of the propositions or contents that sentences provide as consisting of both qualitative propositions, involving only properties, and singular propositions, involving objects. In this view, "Tully was an orator" and "Cicero was an orator" would refer to the same circumstance. Once Frege realized that circumstances do not capture differences in cognitive significance among such pairs of sentences, he abandoned them and developed his theory of sense and reference countenancing only Thoughts or qualitative propositions

But circumstances do something important. They get at what sentences with different cognitive significance, and the beliefs that lead us to regard the sentences as true, *do* have in common. Their truth requires the same objects to have the same properties and stand in the same relations. It is just this that is typically important in communication. If I think you are reliable, I want to believe what you believe about things that matter. I don't care all that much if I believe it in the same way, which if often impossible. You tell me, "I have a pipe wrench." I can't say the same thing with "I have a pipe wrench." And I can't believe it by being in the state you are in. But I can say what you said by saying, "You have a pipe wrench," and I can believe what you told me via the corresponding role or character. Then we part company, and an analogous process occurs within my mind. I can't continue to believe what I have learned about you and your pipe wrench via the role or property corresponding to "You have a pipe wrench" once we are no longer conversing. I believe it in another way, via what I now call a "notion" of you, probably attached to a name and including all sorts of information and probably some misinformation about you. So not only in communication, but also in individual psychology, preserving circumstances across different ways of believing is important. The relation among sentences of having different cognitive significance but referring to the same circumstances, and the corresponding relation between belief states that account for differences in cognitive significance, are of paramount importance.

To shift for a moment to amateur anthropology, it seems to me that it was the need for having a vocabulary and concepts that deal with the needs of information sharing that was probably the origin of the folk theory. We report the attitudes for (at least) two purposes. We use them to explain what people do who believe and desire various things. But we also often use what people believe and say as evidence for our own beliefs. Ken says, "My seminar starts at 3." Assuming he is sincere, the corresponding belief, the likely cause of his saying what he did, also explains his leaving our conversation and heading to class. But also, if Ken believes that, it's probably true. He should know when his seminar starts. We invest a lot of energy in trying to believe what others, who should know, believe and tell us. In this case, what is important is not preserving the *how* but the *what*. That is, what we want to preserve are the *circumstances* or singular propositions they believe. We want to believe that the same things have the same properties and stand in the same relations as they do. Believing it in the same *way* may not be possible and in most cases is not that important.

This amateur anthropological speculation explains why attitude reports focus on *what* is believed rather than working as it sort of seems to philosophers that they should and focussing on *how* things are believed. And it would explain why many of us, after overcoming our initial shock at the thought that Frege might have been wrong about something, came to believe that new theories of reference and singular propositions are getting at something important.

So to understand the concept of belief we inhereted from the folk, we need to understand how belief reports work. Finding the right objects of belief, in Lewis's sense, is important, but it is only part of the job. We also need to understand what the objects of belief, in the ordinary sense, are all about.

I think the added complexity of my scheme allows us to appreciate all that the folk theory bequeathed us. It provides a theory of motivation based on the causal roles the same belief states have in different people at different times. And it provides an account of what different people at different times can share in virtue of being in quite different states.

Now, if we consider Lewis's complete theory, all of this can be accounted for in terms of his various strategies of handling so-called *de re* beliefs. But if we take his whole theory into account, it is, if anything, more elaborate than mine. Thrilled as I was to have an influence on David Lewis, a friend who had taught me a lot, I wasn't convinced that his scheme was preferable.

4   Self-Ascription

As I said, Lewis's paper was written after "Frege on Demonstratives," but about the same time as "The Problem of the Essential Indexical." I was unaware of Lewis's theory, and he was unaware of the second paper in my series. In that second essay, I considered the plausibility of what I called "theories of relativized propositions." Relativized propositions are parametric propositions – i.e., properties with variables for speaker, time, and possibly other elements of context. They pretty much amount to Lewis's properties and do the work of roles in "Frege on Demonstratives." I complained that relativized propositions must be not only believed, but believed in a certain way, the way appropriate to believing when the believer and the time of belief are both the agent and time of the context, and also the person and time at which the relativized proposition is evaluated for truth. Without an account of this way of believing, I said, the relativized-propositions theorist cannot explain the importance of indexicals in expressing beliefs.

Leaving time aside for simplicity, consider the relativized proposition, role, or property corresponding to "x at t has a beard." Someone who doesn't have this property can nevertheless think that others do. To get to a belief that can be true or false, we need not just the property but someone to have it or not have it. I can think that David Lewis has a beard or that I have a beard; the same relativized proposition is involved, but different beliefs. But then we have the problem of the essential indexical. When I say, "I have a beard," I seem to have disclosed a certain sort of belief, different than the kind I have when I say, "David Lewis has a beard." But the difference doesn't simply consist of the identity of the disclosing agent and the subject. For I could regard "JP has a beard" as true while not regarding "I have a beard" as true, as various Castañeda-inspired examples show. Or, to bring time back in, the stipulated non-amnesiac tardy professor can regard "x's department meeting starts at t" as true of the pair consisting of himself and noon, without regarding "My department meeting starts now" as true. So, I argued, the essential indexical is not solved by simply appealing to relativized propositions.

Lewis's theory seems to contain an answer to my objection. We *self-ascribe* properties; belief consists in the self-ascription of properties. But what is self-ascription?

In the interpretation that makes Lewis's view most similar to mine, to self-ascribe a property is simply to be in a belief state the causal role of which is captured by the property. The truth-conditions captured by the property will be relative to the agent and time of the belief and will not be those we focus on when we report the belief. Interpreted this way, Lewis's view is not a version of the doctrine of relativized propositions, for relativized propositions are not *what* is believed. But in this interpretation, "self-ascription" is a bit of misleading terminology. Being in a belief state is one thing; ascribing that belief state to oneself sounds like something quite different. I think chickens and children and nonphilosophers are in belief states that can be usefully classified by roles or classifying properties, but they manage to get by without ascribing such properties to themselves or anyone else.

But there is another way of interpreting Lewis, and, as I said, I think this is the way he is usually interpreted. This involves taking "self-ascription" as a new kind of attitude. Self-ascription is to belief a bit like mass is to weight. Weight is a common-sense concept that depends not only on the nature and constitution of the object that has the weight, but also on external factors; the same thing can have different weights at different elevations, or on the earth and on the moon. Mass is the underlying physical property that we need to understand weight scientifically; it doesn't depend on external circumstances. Similarly, one might think that belief is a sort of useful but confused part of common sense that needs to be properly understood in terms of a more basic attitude, self-ascription.

On this interpretation, Lewis doesn't really give up the doctrine of propositions. Of course, he doesn't think that belief consists in a relation to a proposition. But he thinks it consists in a relation (self-ascription) to another kind of abstract object, properties – not particular exemplifications of properties, but properties abstracted from particular exemplifications. The believer may not have the properties of agents-at-times that classify the causal role of his beliefs; they may never be exemplified by any agent at any time. In this interpretation, Lewis holds that there is an underlying "attitude", self-ascription, and self-ascription is a relation between agents-at-times and properties.

This interpretation is naturally suggested by the phrase "self-ascription." I think the term is a disaster.

Given my preferred interpretation, I agree with a remark of Seth Yalcin quoted by Cappelen and Dever:

> ... talk of "self-ascription" within Lewis's framework is a dispensable heuristic, not something carrying an explanatory load, and not something essential to understanding the proposal. (p. 107)

I would add that heuristic is not only dispensable but harmful. At times, Lewis makes it clear that this is all he really means by "self-ascription."

> The main purpose of assigning objects of attitudes is, I take it, to characterize states of the head; to specify their causal roles with respect to behavior, stimuli, and one another. (Lewis 1979, p. 526)

Given this conception of objects of belief, it seems that all that is required of a believer is to *be in* the states so characterized. No additional *act* of "self-ascription" is required. The believer is in a certain state. The belief anyone has in virtue of being in that state is true if and only if the believer satisfies certain conditions at the time of the belief. The truth of the belief locates the believer and the time of belief relative to the object he has beliefs about; hence, it is in my terminology "self-locating."

Lewis's terminology obscures the important distinction I discussed in the previous chapter, between what I call "agent-relative knowledge" or "primitive self-knowledge" and what I call "self-attached knowledge." A human, or any other animal, that has a self-locating belief (or something like a belief), has primitive self-knowledge. Chickens can have primitive self-knowledge, for they can be in states that constitute beliefs, or some primitive precursor of beliefs, that are true only if the chicken in the state has, say, a kernel of corn in front of her. Chickens do not pass Gallup's mirror test (Gallup 1970). They know that there are other chickens, but they don't seem to regard themselves as one instance of chicken-hood, sharing properties with other chickens, so that they *can* pick up information about themselves in the same way they pick up information about other chickens. If a chicken confronting a kernel of corn could speak English, she wouldn't say, "there is a kernel of corn in front of me now," but "Lo, a kernel of corn." Now I have drifted from amateur anthropology into amateur animal psychology, but perhaps, even if I am being unfair to chickens, my speculations will serve to make the point. Primitive self-knowledge is ubiquitous in the animal kingdom, and states that constitute primitive self-knowledge are essential to survival.

What I call "self-attached knowledge" requires more. It requires a conception of oneself as one among others, of whom the same things may be predicated. In my picture, adult humans have "self-notions," which are the repositories of information gained by perception of their environments, interoception, proprioception, kinesthesia, introspection, and other "normally self-informative" ways of knowing what is going on, plus other information gained in normally other-informative ways, that they have concluded is about the same person they know about these self-informative ways. I claim the use of the first-person requires such self-notions. 'I' and other indexicals are expressions in language that serve the purpose of communicating our beliefs to others, hence they may believe the same things about the same objects and properties as we do, if they are in a position to determine their references. They are tools of communication. Merely having a self-locating belief does not require all that is required to use indexicals for this purpose.

If you tell me, "You have a bug on your shoulder," I will think that what you said is true if the person you are addressing has a bug on their shoulder. If I think you are addressing me, then that the person you are addressing is the one I know about when I perceive, interocept, and the like. If I think you are reliable, I will go into a belief state whose causal role can be helpfully characterized by the property of having a bug on one's shoulder. Since I am a reasonably competent adult, this belief will be added to my self-notion, at least until I flick off the bug. This is this sort of transaction that "self-ascription" suggests. But then self-ascribing a property isn't simply being in a belief state whose causal role is classified by the property. The term "self-ascription" suggests a confusion or conflation that, in my analysis, is not intrinsic to Lewis's theory. The term "*de se*" is also confusing in my opinion, as it invites the same conflation.

So, I think there are two interpretations Lewis. The one I prefer makes his view closest to mine:

My preferred interpretation of Lewis

Properties of individuals at times can be used to classify belief-states in a way that captures their causal roles.

De se beliefs are beliefs the truth of which puts conditions on the believer and time of belief, thus the same as my "self-locating beliefs".

Not all beliefs are self-locating or *de se*.

If one considers "logical space" as well as location in space and time, one can introduce broader notions of self-locating and *de se* belief. I will call them "*de se**" and "self-locating*". All beliefs are self-locating* and *de se**. This makes no sense outside the possible worlds framework, and since Lewis doesn't use '*' is confusing even if one does.

To say that one "self-ascribes" a property is simply a misleading way of saying that one is in a belief state the causal role of which is captured by the property. Self-ascription is not a newly discovered attitude.

To say that properties are the "objects of belief" is simply another misleading way of saying the same thing.

The more common interpretation of Lewis

Beliefs consist in a person at a time self-ascribing a property of the sort that persons may have at times in worlds.

The belief is true IFF the person has the self-ascribed property at the time of self-ascription in the world of self-ascription.

The facts of self-ascription are established by what goes on in the head. The self-ascribed properties are in the head. Facts outside of the head may be relevant to the semantics of belief-reports, but not the structure of belief.

A *de se* belief is one the truth of which puts conditions on the believer, time, and world of self-ascription and hence locates the agent in logical space. All beliefs are *de se*.

Beliefs that do not locate the agent and time of belief in physical space are *de dicto*.

There are no *de re* beliefs. The term is just a misleading way of characterizing cases in which the *de se* or *de dicto* belief puts certain kinds of conditions on the objects that need to have various properties and stand in various relations for the belief to be true.

I'm inclined to prefer both my scheme and my terminology, and I would prefer to think that the first interpretation is Lewis's view, and his terminology is misleading. But it's hard to be sure.

13

The View From Everywhere

As I read Cappelen and Dever's book, it seemed to transform from an annoyingly unfair and inaccurate critique of my views into sort of an intriguing mystery novel. What are the views that motivate what they say? What is their view of semantics? Of opacity or the appearance of it? Of how names refer and why there are no important differences between names and indexicals when it comes to cognitive significance? They don't tell us. How do they think of action? They sketch a theory, definitely revisionary in containing no account of the *by* and *way of* relations central to most accounts, but then they disavow it. What are they thinking of with "indexical content" and similar terms of art they introduce? Do they really think that only necessary truths are philosophically deep or epistemologically interesting? What is the unrevised theory of content to which they see my account as a revision? What do *they* mean by "the *de se*"?

In a mystery novel, everything is made clear in the last chapter. But for me, the mystery was simply deepened.

In "Frege on Demonstratives" and "The Problem of the Essential Indexical," I argued that by unburdening propositions, we could retain the thesis that the 'that'-clauses are indirect discourse and attitude reports can be objective propositions – true or false independently of who believes them, where, and when. They can be Fregean Thoughts or some modern version thereof, or singular propositions, both encoding objective, context-independent information, independent of who believes or when. The goal of these essays, not to mention many of the later essays in *The Problem of the Essential Indexical*, is to explain how such an objective picture of the world is arrived at and handled by creatures who have a certain position in space and time that determines what they experience, and the effects of what they do. The goal is to assess how such an objective conception of what is perceived, believed, desired, and accomplished is consistent with gaining information in context-dependent ways (and often expressing it in context-dependent ways) and being motivated by the information to perform actions – the results of which depend on context but are themselves as objective as any other facts.

So I might summarize my view as:

> ... contents are, and are used as, tools for representing (and, of course, sometimes misrepresenting) the objective state of the world.

But this is a quote from Cappelen and Dever; this is *their* view. Where is the difference? This quote is surrounded by:

> But we also think the substantive conclusion of the tradition is wrong, and that there is no deep or philosophically interesting notion of perspectival content. [...] Some of the states represented are "perspectival" in the minimal sense that they are facts about our immediate environment, or facts about how things are in relation to us. Some of our representational systems are indexical in the minimal (Kaplanian) sense that they represent as they do in part in virtue of where they are situated in the world. But there's nothing more to the phenomenon than that – fundamentally, all information is objective information, and is used indifferently by us as such. (p. 173)

I don't like, or even understand, some of the phrases here, like "deep or philosophically interesting." I guess I just have low standards. And I don't know what they mean by "perspectival content," although I could put some effort in coming up with such a notion, along the lines of indexical, nominal, and referential contents. I don't know why the fact that some representational systems are "indexical" in the Kaplanian sense is so unimportant and presumably shallow and philosophically uninteresting. Indexicals and Kaplan's theory, and understanding how such "indexical" representational systems tie into our conception of an objective world, quickened my sense of the queer, and it's too bad they don't find it interesting. I'm sorry they had to spend so much time worrying about my views on uninteresting topics they find shallow – although I think once they resolved to do so, they should have spent a little more time, expended a bit more effort, and done a better job of it. But, aside from such verbiage, I don't understand what they think they are disagreeing with me about.

The rest of their chapter, if one brackets verbiage about philosophical depth and the like, mostly consists of fairly reasonable platitudes about our human conception of an objective world and how it plays into our deepest desires for other people and the future of the world. What it doesn't provide is an account of how this objective conception, important to the human condition, evolved from the basic animal condition, or ties into methods humans also rely on to find out about the world, or the context-sensitive ways we often express and communicate such information – issues on which I think my views shed some light.

So at the end of the book, the mysteries still remain. I think the confusion and conflation of many senses of "content" throughout the book is a large part of the problem. And, as Falk points out:

> Cappelen and Dever have confused perspectival properties (or predicates if there are no such properties) with acts of self-ascription, as if one if and only if the other. It is a wonder, given their own appeal for objective properties in their last chapter, that they would not see the essential indexical is about locating oneself, not in a seeming-world, but in the objectively real world. (2015)

But these are diagnoses, not interpretations. There is no explanation of the semantics of sentences, or indirect discourse, or attitude reports, or of the structure of action, or of how information gained in context-sensitive ways can be integrated with objective information, or how the combination motivates rational action in some way in which the causal roles of internal states mesh with their objective contents – issues on which I toiled, apparently in the uninteresting shallows of philosophy, to explain. It is clear that they firmly believe in an objective world.

It is a bit as if, at the end of an Agatha Christie novel, Miss Marple gathers everyone together, but instead of solving the mystery, she sings "God Save the Queen."

14

Conclusion

Early on, Cappelen and Dever say,

> ... there is no such thing as essential indexicality, irreducibly *de se* attitudes, or self-locating attitudes. Our goal is not to show that we need to rethink these phenomena – that they should be explained in ways different from how, e.g., Lewis and Perry explained them. Our goal is to show that the entire topic is an illusion – there's nothing there. (p. 3)

They go on to list many astute philosophers, far brighter than I, who have been taken in by my "rhetoric" and the arguments I "paraded" to accept "essential indexicality." Of course the list starts with Lewis; it continues with Dennett and Recanati and many other exemplars of philosophical brilliance. This raises the question, why were they so deceived? Can my rhetoric really be that good? I suggest a more plausible explanation. There was something right about what I said; these philosophers read my essays more carefully than Cappelen and Dever did, and recognized it.

Bibliography

Almog, Joseph, John Perry, and Howard Wettstein, eds. 1989. *Themes from Kaplan*. New York: Oxford University Press.

Anscombe, G. E. M. 1975. "The First Person." In *Mind and Language*, edited by Samuel Guttenplan, 45–65. Oxford: Clarendon Press.

Atkins, Philip. 2016. "Review of Cappelen and Dever, The Inessential Indexical." *Analysis Review* 76:99–102.

Barwise, Jon, and John Perry. 1999. *Situations and Attitudes*. Stanford: CSLI Publications. Reprint, with additions, of *Situations and Attitudes*. MIT Press, 1983.

Burge, Tyler. 1979. "Individualism and the Mental." *Midwest Studies In Philosophy* 4:73–121.

Cappelen, Herman, and Josh Dever. 2013. *The Inessential Indexical: On the Philosophical Insignificance of Perspective and the First Person*. Oxford University Press.

Castañeda, Hector Neri. 1999. *The Phenomeno-Logic of the I: Essays on Self-Consciousness*. First Edition edition. Edited by James G. Hart and Tomis Kapitan. Bloomington: Indiana University Press.

Castañeda, Hector-Neri. 1966. "'He': A Study in the Logic of Self-Consciousness." *Ratio* 8 (December): 130–57.

———. 1967. "Indicators and Quasi-Indicators." *American Philosophical Quarterly* 4 (2): 85–100.

———. 1968. "On the Logic of Attributions of Self-Knowledge to Others." *Journal of Philosophy* 65 (15): 439–456.

Corazza, Eros. 2004. *Reflecting the Mind: Indexicality and Quasi-indexicality*. Oxford University Press.

Corazza, Eros, and Kepa Korta. 2015. "Frege on Subject Matter and Identity Statements." *Analysis* 75 (4): 562–65.

Crimmins, Mark. 1992. *Talk About Beliefs*. Cambridge, Mass: MIT Press.

Crimmins, Mark, and John Perry. 1989. "The Prince and the Phone Booth: Reporting Puzzling Beliefs." *Journal of Philosophy* 86 (12): 685–711. Reprinted in *The Problem of the Essential Indexical and Other Essays*. Expanded Edition. Stanford: CSLI Publications, 2000.

De Ponte, María. 2017. "Promises, the Present and 'now.' Lessons from Austin, Prior and Kamp." *Journal of Pragmatics* 112.

De Ponte, Maria, and Kepa Korta. 2017. "New Thoughts about Old Facts: On Prior's Root Canal." In *Reference and Representation in Thought and Language*. Oxford: Oxford University Press.

De Ponte, María, Kepa Korta, and John Perry. Forthcoming. "Four Puzzling Paragraphs: Frege on '≡' and '='."

Dennett, Daniel C. 1981. "Where Am I." In *Brainstorms: Philosophical Essays on Mind and Psychology*. Cambridge, Mass.: The MIT Press.

Donnellan, Keith S. 1966. "Reference and Definite Descriptions." *Philosophical Review* 75 (3): 281–304.

———. 1970. "Proper Names and Identifying Descriptions." *Synthese* 21 (3-4): 335–58.

Dretske, Fred. 1986. "Misrepresentation." In *Belief: Form, Content, and Function*, edited by Radu J. Bogdan, 17–36. Oxford University Press.

Durant, Will. 1961. *The Story of Philosophy*. Simon and Schuster.

Falk, Arthur. 2015. "Hermann Cappelen and Josh Dever, The Inessential Indexical: On the Philosophical Insignificance of Perspective and the First Person." *Journal of the Indian Council of Philosophical Research* 32 (3): 425–430.

Frege, Gottlob. 1879. *Begriffschrift, Eine Der Arithmetischen Nachgebildete Formelsprache Des Reinen Denkens*. Halle: L. Nerbert.

———. 1884. *Grundlagen Der Arithmetik. Eine Logisch Mathematische Untersuchung Über Den Begriff Der Zahl*. Breslau: Wilhelm Koebner.

———. 1893–. 1903. *Grundgesetze der Arithmetik, Band I (1893); Band 2 (1903)*. Jena: Verlag von Hermann Pohle.

———. 1956. "The Thought: A Logical Inquiry." Translated by Peter Geach. *Mind* 65 (259): 289–311. First published in *Beiträge zur Philosophie des Deutschen Idealismus*. 1918-19.

———. 1960a. "Function and Concept." In *Translations from the Philosophical Writings of Gottlob Frege*, 2nd ed., edited by Peter Geach and Max Black, 56–78. Oxford: Blackwell. Originally appeared as *Funktion Und Begriff*. Jena: H. Pohle, 1891.

———. 1960b. "On Sense and Reference." In *Translations from the Philosophical Writings of Gottlob Frege*, 2nd ed., edited and translated by Peter Geach and Max Black, 56–78. Oxford: Blackwell. Originally appeared as *Über Sinn und Bedeutung*. In *Zeitschrift für Philosophie und philosophische Kritik*. 100: 25-50, 1892.

———. 1960c. *Translations from the Philosophical Writings of Gottlob Frege*. 2nd ed. Edited by Peter Geach and Max Black. Oxford: Blackwell. Originally published in 1952.

———. 1980. *Philosophical and Mathematical Correspondence of Gottlob Frege*. Edited by Gottfried Gabriel, H. Hermes, F. Kambartel, Christian Thiel, and Albert Veraart. Chicago: University of Chicago Press. Abridged from the German edition by Brian McGuiness and trans. by Hans Kaal.

———. 2002. "Begriffsschrift, a Formula Language, Modeled upon That of Arithmetic, for Pure Thought." In *From Frege to Godel: A Source Book in Mathematical Logic, 1879-1931*, 1st edition, edited by Jean van Heijenoort, translated by Stefan Bauer-Mengelberg, 1–82. Cambridge, Mass: Harvard University Press. This essay originally appeared as *Begriffsschrift, eine der arithmetischen nachgebildete Formelsprache des reinen Denkens*. Halle: L. Nerbert, 1079.

French, Peter A., Theodore Edward Uehling, and Howard K. Wettstein, eds. 1979. *Contemporary Perspectives in the Philosophy of Language*. Minneapolis: University of Minnesota Press.

Gallup, Gordon. 1970. "Chimpanzees: Self-Recognition." *Science* 167 (January 2): 86–87.

Grice, Paul. 1975. "Logic and Conversation." In *Syntax and Semantics, Volume 3: Speech Acts*, edited by Peter Cole and Jerry L. Morgan, 41–58. New York: Academic Press.

Hall, Lisa Louise. 1994. "Individualism, Mental Content and Cognitive Science." PhD Thesis, Stanford University.

Hinzen, Wolfram. 2015. "Review of Cappelen and Dever, *The Inessential Indexical*." *Mind* 124:898–904.

Israel, David, and John Perry. 1990. "What Is Information?" In *Information, Language, and Cognition*, edited by Philip P. Hanson, 1:1–19. Vancouver Studies in Cognitive Science. Vancouver: University of British Columbia Press.

———. 1991. "Information and Architecture." In *Situation Theory and Its Applications*, edited by Jon Barwise, Jean Mark Gawron, Gordon Plotkin, and Syun Tutiya, 2:147–60. CSLI Lecture Notes 26. Stanford: CSLI Publications.

Kaplan, David. 1979a. "Dthat." In *Contemporary Perspectives in the Philosophy of Language*, edited by Peter A. French, Theodore Edward Uehling, and Howard K. Wettstein, 383–400. Minneapolis: University of Minnesota Press.

———. 1979b. "On the Logic of Demonstratives." In *Contemporary Perspectives in the Philosophy of Language*, edited by Peter A. French, Theodore Edward Uehling, and Howard K. Wettstein, 401–412. Minneapolis: University of Minnesota Press.

———. 1989. "Demonstratives: An Essay on the Semantics, Logic, Metaphysics and Epistemology of Demonstratives and Other Indexicals." In *Themes From Kaplan*, edited by Joseph Almog, John Perry, and Howard Wettstein, 481–563. Oxford University Press.

Korta, Kepa, and John Perry. 2011. *Critical Pragmatics: An Inquiry into Reference and Communication*. Cambridge: Cambridge University Press.

Kretzmann, Norman. 1966. "Omniscience and Immutability." *Journal of Philosophy* 63 (14): 409–421.

Kripke, Saul A. 1979. "A Puzzle About Belief." In *Meaning and Use*, edited by A. Margalit, 239–83. Dordrecht: D. Reidel.

Kripke, Saul A. 1980. *Naming and Necessity*. Cambridge, Mass: Harvard University Press. First published in Davidson, Donald and Harman, Gilbert, eds., *Semantics of Natural Language*. Dordrecht: Reidel: 253-355, 763-69, 1972.

———. 2008. "Frege's Theory of Sense and Reference: Some Exegetical Notes." *Theoria* 74 (3): 181–218.

———. 2011. "The First Person." In *Philosophical Troubles: Collected Papers*, 1:292–320. New York: Oxford University Press.

Lewis, David. 1966. "An Argument for the Identity Theory." *The Journal of Philosophy* 63:17–25.

———. 1979. "Attitudes De Dicto and De Se." *The Philosophical Review* 88 (4): 513–543.

Lima, Juliana Faccio. 2018. "Indexicality and Action: Why We Need Indexical Beliefs to Motivate Intentional Actions." *Inquiry:* 1–21.

McTaggart, J. Ellis. 1908. "The Unreality of Time." *Mind* 17 (68): 457–74.

Morris, Charles. 1946. *Signs, Language and Behavior*. Signs, Language and Behavior. Oxford, England: Prentice-Hall.

Perry, John. 1977. "Frege on Demonstratives." *Philosophical Review* 86 (4): 474–97. Reprinted in *The Problem of the Essential Indexical and Other Essays*. Expanded Edition. Stanford: CSLI Publications, 2000.

———. 1979. "The Problem of the Essential Indexical." *Noûs* 13:3–21. Reprinted in *The Problem of the Essential Indexical and Other Essays*. Expanded Edition. Stanford: CSLI Publications, 2000.

———. 1980. "Belief and Acceptance." *Midwest Studies in Philosophy* 5 (1): 533–42. Reprinted in *The Problem of the Essential Indexical and Other Essays*. Expanded Edition. Stanford: CSLI Publications, 2000.

———. 1998. "Myself and 'I'." In *Philosophie in Synthetischer Absicht*, edited by Marcelo Stamm, 83–103.

———. 2000. *The Problem of the Essential Indexical and Other Essays*. Expanded Edition. Stanford: CSLI Publications.

———. 2011. *Reference and Reflexivity*. 2nd ed. Stanford: CSLI Publications.

———. 2017. "Indexicals and Undexicals." In *Reference and Representation in Thought and Language*, edited by Maria de Ponte and Kepa Korta. Oxford: Oxford University Press.

———. 2019. *Frege's Detour: An Essay on Meaning, Reference, and Truth*. Oxford: Oxford University Press.

Prior, Arthur. 1959. "Thank Goodness That's Over." *Philosophy* 34 (128): 12–17.

Recanati, François. 1993. *Direct Reference: From Language to Thought*. Oxford: Blackwell.

———. 2007. *Perspectival Thought: A Plea for Moderate Relativism*. Oxford ; New York: Clarendon Press.

———. 2012. *Mental Files*. Oxford: Oxford University Press.

———. 2016. *Mental Files in Flux*. Oxford: Oxford University Press.

Richard, Mark. 1983. "Direct Reference and Ascriptions of Belief." *Journal of Philosophical Logic* 12 (4): 425–52.

Salmon, Nathan U. 1986. *Frege's Puzzle*. Atascadero, CA: Ridgeview Publishing.

Schwitzgebel, Eric. 2019. "Belief." In *The Stanford Encyclopedia of Philosophy*, Fall 2019 Edition, edited by Edward N. Zalta. Metaphysics Research Lab, Stanford University.

Shoemaker, Sydney. 1963. *Self-Knowledge and Self Identity*. First Edition edition. Ithaca: Cornell University Press.

———. 1968. "Self-Reference and Self-Awareness." *Journal of Philosophy* 65:555–67.

Soames, Scott. 1985. "Lost Innocence." *Linguistics and Philosophy* 8 (1): 59–71.

Wettstein, Howard. 1986. "Has Semantics Rested on a Mistake?" *The Journal of Philosophy* 83 (4): 185–209.

Yalcin, Seth. 2012. "Stanley on the De Se." Pacific Meeting of the American Philosophical Association, Chicago, April 5.

Index